AF560011

EDUCATIONAL PHILOSOPHY OF JOHN DEWEY

EDUCATIONAL PHILOSOPHY OF JOHN DEWEY

By

Dr. D. Vijaya Bharathi

M.A., M.A., M.Ed., M.Phil., Ph.D
Lecturer
St. Joseph's College of Education for Women
Guntur, Andhra Pradesh

Editor

Dr. Digumarti Bhaskara Rao

M.Sc., M.A., M.A., M.Ed., Ph.D.
Reader
R.V.R. College of Education, Guntur
Member
Board of Studies in Education
Acharya Nagarjuna University

DISCOVERY PUBLISHING HOUSE
NEW DELHI-110002

First Published - 2005

Reprinted - 2017

ISBN: 978-81-8356-024-5

Educational Philosophy of John Dewey

Published by:

DISCOVERY PUBLISHING HOUSE PVT. LTD.

4383/4B, Ansari Road, Darya Ganj

New Delhi-110 002 (India)

Phone: +91-11-23279245, 43596064-65

Fax: +91-11-23253475

E-mail: discoverypublishinghouse@gmail.com

sales@discoverypublishinggroup.com

web: www.discoverypublishinggroup.com

Printed at:

Infinity Imaging Systems

Delhi

Preface

John Dewey, the legendary educationist, is remembered in the classrooms everyday everywhere due to his wonderful contributions to the field of education. His pragmatism and laboratory school are the exemplary examples of his greatest contributions.

The educational philosophy of John Dewey is explained in this book with the headings Philosophy of Life, Education, Aims of Education, Methods of Teaching and Learning, Teacher, Curriculum, Discipline and Values along with his biography.

This book on the educational philosophy of John Dewey would be very much useful to educationists, teachers, students, parents and researchers.

—Dr. Bhaskara Rao Digumarti

"Sai Soudha"
D-43, S.V.N. Colony
Guntur–522 006
Andhra Pradesh

Contents

Contents

1

Introduction

"The art of education would never attain clearness in itself without philosophy, there is an interaction between the two and either without the other is incomplete and unserviceable". Fitche.

The most sacred of all creations of God is the human life and it has two aspects—one biological and other sociological. If nutrition and reproduction maintain and transmit the biological aspects, the sociological aspect is transmitted by education. Man is primarily distinguishable from the animals because of power of reasoning. Man is endowed with intelligence, remains active, original and energetic. Man lives in accordance with his philosophy of life and his conception of the world.

What is Education?

Education is an important social activity planned and shared by the parents and the society. Education is a process of learning to live the life of a community. Education has been defined by different people in different ways. The meaning of education has been changing according to people, places and times. Some took education to mean the process, others the results, still others the methodology. Since the concept has changed the definitions have also changed. Yet, there are certain definitions, which are all time popular and also acceptable. Aristotle has defined education as "creation of a sound mind in a sound body". But this we can understand that education should pay attention to our physical needs and also to the mental needs. Pastalozzi defined education as "a natural harmonious and progressive development of man's innate powers". By saying so, Pestalozzi has made the factors heredity and environment and their role in the personality development very clear. Mahatma Gandhi wrote, "By education, I mean an allround drawing out of the best in child and man-body, mind and spirit". By this, we can very well understand that the Mahatma wants a harmonious development of the various faculties of human beings.

A comprehensive definition of education must take into consideration a few factors. They are (i) the individual who is to be educated, and (ii) the society in which education is to take place. Education can be best described as "the nurture of personal growth". When education is considered as the conservation transmission and renewal of entire culture, then it becomes an instrument by which a community maintains itself.

What is Philosophy?

The list of achievement of human beings is very long and it is a big question to all philosophers. How has man achieved all that he has achieved? How has all this been done? Philosophy endeavours to understand all that comes within the bounds of human experience. It aims at the fundamental understanding of things, the problem of human conduct, the assumptions that underlie religious and scientific beliefs, the tools and methods of thinking or any issue that arises in any field of human activity. Philosophy seeks to provide a complete account of man's world, which is reflective and critical in nature. Philosophy wants to understand man in relation to the whole universe, nature and God. Philosophy deals with the nature of the human mind and personality and the ways in which man and all his institutions can be understood. Philosophy seeks to understand whether man is free or within bondage and whether he can change the course of history. Philosophy, therefore, may be understood as a search for a comprehensive view of nature, an attempt at universal explanation of the nature of things. Philosophy gives man that knowledge and wisdom with the help of which he understands the whole universe and the implications of the same or relations to himself and all the people around. Philosophy is a consistent search for the consistent explanation of different realities around us. The eternal quest for truth lends the origin of philosophy. A love of wisdom is the essence for any philosophic investigation.

Philosophy has been defined by various scholars from various angles. The literal meaning of philosophy is live of wisdom. The word philosophy originated from the Greek language. The wise men of Greece had raised a number of questions about the origin of the universe, life and creation. It must be noted that philosophy is not anyone's belief or point of view concerning purposes or values. On the other hand, philosophy is a rigorous, disciplined and guarded analysis of some of the most difficult problems which man has faced. Philosophers are men of great intelligence and remarkable insight, who have been able to see the significance of the discreet events in human experiences.

Betrand Russel opines that "Philosophy is to be studied not for the sake of any definite answers to it's question, but rather for the sake of the questions themselves, because these questions enlarge our conceptions of what is possible but above all because—the mind also becomes capable of that union, with the universe, which constitutes its highest good". Needless to say philosophers differ in their answers to various eternal questions of life and there is no one philosophy which all of us may follow; yet every philosophy will enable us to derive knowledge of some kind. Philosophy as such is a mature reflection about any problem in its complete perspective. Some people regard it as an intellectual luxury but in fact it is life's necessity. Philosophy helps us to understand the significance of all human experiences and activity. The deepest questions of life are clarified by philosophy. Such a clarification is most essential if we do not want to lead a life of confusion and conflict, ambiguity and inconsistency. Philosophy is the supreme instrument by which man comes to terms with himself as he struggles to organise his existence within culture.

Several great thinkers have defined philosophy in many ways. In Coleridge defined philosophy as "the science of all sciences", Cisaro called it "the mother of all arts and true medicine of mind". Both Alexander and Kant felt that philosophy is metaphysics. Philosophy, according to Alexander, is an attempt to study such comprehensive topics like reality and universe—he combines two concepts metaphysics and criticism in his philosophy. Kant also agrees with Alexander and further adds that philosophy should give up the attempt to know the ultimate realities like God and the self, and limit itself to the world of experience. Plato states that the knowledge of reality is a knowledge of the universe, unchangeable and eternal. Such knowledge cannot be given sense perception which does not reveal the reality of things but gives mere appearances.

What is Educational Philosophy?

Man philosophises whenever he tries to express his belief and its various aspects. Education is one of the most important aspects of life. So whoever has tried to philosophise education has been called an educational philosopher or thinker. Philosophy, whether explicit or implicit, is always in the background for shaping things in education. It answers thousands of questions pertaining to the field of education. The importance of education is enormous. The over all meaning of education is given by Redden, "education is the deliberate and systematic influence exerted by the mature person upon the immature person through instruction and discipline. It means the harmonious development of all powers of the human being—physical, social, intellectual, aesthetic and spiritual. The essential elements in the educative process are a creative mind, a well-integrated self, socially useful purposes and experiences related to the interests, needs and abilities of the individual as a participant or social being". The chief task of philosophy is to determine what constitutes a life worth living—the chief task of education on the other hand is to make life worth living. Therefore, philosophy tells the essentials and goals of good life and education gives the means to achieve those goals and learn those essentials of good life. Philosophy is the contemplative and education is the active side of life. Education is nothing but applied philosophy. Philosophy deals with the abstract whereas education deals with the concrete. Both of them go together.

Whether it is East or West, philosophy determines all the broad aspects of education. So long as we need aims of education, based on philosophy and based on the ultimate goals of life, this need will always be there. Philosophy will continue influencing and determining both the matter and the method of education. It will continue making a unique contribution to the development of the educational theory and practice. Modern philosophers have also a special impact. In the 19th century, there was the influence of the concept of mechanism on physics, psychology and economics. Neo-Darwinism gave rise to the acceptance of the principles of struggle for existence, cut throat competition, gradual process of adaptation of life, purposiveness of life, intellectualism and men's faith in reason. Emphasis of knowledge received universal acceptance. In the 20th century, the two world wars and the consequent mass destruction brought by the application of science, gave rise to loss of faith in mere intellect. Humanism, faith in higher principles and values of life, character development and emotional integration received greater impetus. There began a distrust of mere logic. New schools of philosophy originated, trying to synthesise science and religion and that is almost a synthesis of pragmatism and idealism. The present age is an age of reunion, the period of synthesis both in philosophy and in education. Philosophy not only lays down the ends, but also wishes that the means must constantly look to the ends so that they may not be leading astray.

All great philosophers are great educationists. Thales in Greece, Confucius in China, Buddha and Gandhi in India and many more have all reflected their philosophical views in their educational schemes. For example, Plato's idealism brought forth his cultural schemes of education. Rousseau's anti-social philosophy was reflected in his 'negative natural education', and Dewey's philosophy has resulted in the modern 'Project Method'. Truths and principles established by philosophy are applied in the conduct of educative process—several schools of thought have come into vogue, like, Idealism, Naturalism, Pragmatism, Realism,

Humanism and many more. Such schools of thought have cropped up because philosophers differ in their answers to several questions of life. Despite all the differences, philosophers have all agreed on one point that education is the means to achieve life's ambitions and goals.

Retrospects and Perspectives

History tells us that most primitive tribes viewed education as a means for securing social solidarity and uniformity. During the medieval period education was used to serve political and religious ends. The Renaissance effected a change in the whole outlook of life and education was recorded as a means for independent personal culture and individual development. At first, the Reformation was a continuation of the best educational influences of Renaissance. But, many aspects of a new formalism crept into the educational practices, which are little different from the mediaeval scholasticism with realistic tendencies. During the seventeenth century we find the beginnings of the psychological, scientific and sociological movements in education which are trying to reach their peak today. There are three fundamental things in life—Mind (the self), Matter (the physical world) and Experience. A thinker who idolises the "mind and the self" is an idealist. One who emphasises "reality, matter and physical world" is called a materialist. One who refuses to speculate and transcends beyond experience is called a pragmatist. Each one of these Schools of Philosophy analyses and interprets the different aspects of education in its own specialised way.

Man has two facets—spiritual and material. When the emphasis is on the realisation of spirituality, life is called idealism. An idealist does not have considerations for material values of life. To him, spiritual world is the manifestation of some great spirit behind it, while the material and physical world is destructable and changeable. To the idealists 'Mind and Soul' are more important than the 'Matter and the Body'. The idealists do not regard environment, physical or social, primarily responsible for creating a man. If scientists and artists have given us some masterpieces, they were not the results of reactions to a certain physical stimulus but they were characteristic creations of mind. 'Exalt the human personality' is the core of the philosophy of idealism. According to Ross "Human personality is of supreme value and constitutes the noblest work of God". The development of personality therefore has been given the first position in idealist philosophy. Mind is totally idolised by the idealists. Believing in the theory of evolution, they advocate the evolution of the mind which is responsible for the progressive nature of man and the world. Mind is the creator of the new and the explainer of the existing phenomena. Man's works are due to his powers of symbolic thinking. The full evolution of mind enables man to know the truth and avoid the error, to appreciate beauty and avoid ugliness, to expose goodness and avoid evil. Truth, goodness and beauty are the spiritual ideals for which man should aspire and strive. This is the task of the idealists. Knowledge through the activity of mind rather than through senses is the first article of faith in idealism. Intelligence, creativity and dynamism of man differentiate him from other animals. Through the use of these powers man creates cultural environment. Another article of faith with the idealists is the emancipation of the spirit. They attach no importance to life of flesh, they are the high priests of life of spirit. Man's spiritual nature is the key essence of his being and he must create a spiritual environment, which is endowed with the choicest benedictions of God. The third essence of idealism is the realisation of higher values of life. Their ideals are to be discovered by man. Heaven lies about us and not above us. Life is glorious, hence it is to be lived in a glorified manner. Idealists believe that there is a divine power behind all things good in the world. A man's rational self is superior to every other self, physical and emotional. It is the rational self which discovers the truth.

The human personality grows because of the interaction of the personality with the environment. The Puritan settlers of America had to face many problems in creating their own civilization in those new environments. They possessed no readymade solutions for those problems. Old ideas would not help them. So they experimented upon many new ideas and adopted those which proved useful for them in solving their day-to-day problems. Consequently they built up a philosophy of life, based on their own experiments and experiences. They came to the conclusion that values are not fixed in advance. They are man-made. In the words of John Dewey, the father of Pragmatism, and in and out American Philosophy, "Values are as unstable as the forms of clouds. They keep on changing from time to time and reality is still in the process of making. Ideal ends are remotely connected with immediate and urgent conditions. Men naturally devote themselves to the present conditions rather than the remote". According to pragmatism, whatever fulfils man's purposes and desires and develops his life is true. Truth is that which gives satisfactory results when put into practice. A pragmatist believes in practical and utilitarian philosophy. He believes that man has the power to shape his environment to his own needs. The world is changing and nothing is true or good forever. What was good yesterday may cease to be good today. The old order changeth yielding place to new and one good custom may corrupt the world after some time. Pragmatism believes in change—hence it does not accept the existence of any static quality or virtue. Pragmatism in education is against armchair theorising and hair spliting tendencies of traditional philosophers. Its theory of education is based upon close relationship between theory and practice of education. Our society is changing and dynamic. Very rapid changes are taking place and conditions of life are not static. Pragmatic education is progressive education, which stands for flexibility, change and adaptability. It advocates freedom and worth of the individual personality and the ideals accepted by a society at one particular time to maintain it's existence.

Man is a purposive being with the essential nature of approving or disapproving nature, appreciating or criticising everything that he sees, does and feels. Everything in life makes its multiple impacts on man for better or worse. Everyone has needs, urges and aspirations, and anything that fulfils the needs, satisfies the urges and helps on in realising the aspirations has a value. Our conduct and attitude towards objects, ideals and persons, depends upon the values. These objects, persons and ideals have for us. Everything, therefore, is of value to man and he has been making efforts to evaluate as validity and as wisely as possible for him. Man does the evaluation every day, every hour, throughout his life.

Values are the fruits which accrue from an activity in pursuit of some goal, in the realisation of certain aims in life we realise certain values. These values are experiences in the course of the fulfilment of our aims. The aim may be one but many values may be realised. For a long time, values were approached philosophically after long deliberation, meditation and reflection and they were determined. "To value" in the words of one great philosophy means "primarily to prize to esteem to appraise, to estimate". It means "the act of cherishing something, holding it dear and also the act of passing judgement upon the nature and amount of its values as compared with something else". If the art of valuing means liking or desiring, then value may be object of any interest. Value is a person's idea of what is desirable, what he and others want, not necessarily what he actually wants. Ideal values are eternal. They flow from the spiritual nature of man. The spirit has moral, intellectual and aesthetic activities. These activities are inspired by the corresponding desires. "Satyam, Shivam, Sundaram" are the attributes of the Supreme Being. The love of God means the love of these divine attributes. Religion, which is the love of God, includes the love of these spiritual values. It is here that we seek the help of education, one of the most powerful instruments to cultivate values in the youth.

There can be no two opinions that education, as an organised social system, has an important function in the development of moral, spiritual and aesthetic values. Education is a process of bringing about desirable changes of behaviour in a learner, in the way he thinks, feels and acts in accordance with our concept of good life. The various goals of education, development of human resources, creativity, commitment to human values and social justice, national cohesion, scientific temper, independence of mind and spirit, socialism, secularism, democracy are no more than educational expressions of our concept of good life. It is through education that society seeks to preserve and promote values.

In the content of education, values have got a narrow meaning and also a wide meaning. In the narrow sense educational values are co-terminus with educational aims. In the wider sense, however, values influence every aspect of the educational process, technique, policy and procedure. Apart from instructional aims, the questions of teaching methods, the motivation for learning, the selection of curriculum, the use of text books, the type of discipline, the administration and supervision and questions of values. There is always some values which arouses and sustains and perpetuates interests of learning. Values determine what we should do and how we should do. We always feel interested in those values which make a difference in our lives and which we can progressively explore and apprehend. The realisation of values stimulates us to make effort. The values which retain the sap of flexibility have sufficient vitality to survive in this constantly evolving world. Dynamism of thought will constantly demand a revaluation and reinterpretation of values.

The growing concern over the erosion values and an increasing cynicism in the society has brought to focus the need for readjustments in the curriculum in order to make education a forceful took for the cultivation of values—social and moral. If values are woven into the very concept of education where is the need for separate value education? It is true that all good education is, in essence, a process of developing the human personality, in all its dimensions—intellectual, physical, social, moral and spiritual. When we talk of value education we should essentially mean the development of social, moral, aesthetic and spiritual sides of the human personality and not merely transformation of information. We are also passing through a phase in our social and political life which poses a special danger to the long accepted values. Values like secularism, socialism, democracy and professional ethics are coming under increasing strain. Population increase has seriously affected the quality of life. Crime, violence and indifference to human suffering have spread to all walks of life. Both physical and social pollution are effecting our lives. The world today faces a catastrophe, as never before in the history of man-kind and we are in need of peace and understanding. All these problems cannot be solved in a piece-meal effort, educational or social. What we need is a drastic change in the very outlook of man in his own life, values and environment. This calls for a deliberate thrust on values in our life, through education.

The East and West have contributed to the philosophy of values. The concept of values is very important in education. It is only what is valuable that is transmitted to the younger generation by the elder generation. The concept of education is to be visualised as nothing but a set of values in essence. R.S. Peters has stated in his 'Ethics and Education' the following as one of the criteria for education. "Education implies the transmission of what is worthwhile in those who become committed to it". According to Harry Schofield value is "what a particular society values so highly that it finds it important to pass it on to each succeeding generations". Hence, what is deemed to be valuable only becomes the content of education. So it is obvious that values and education are correlated.

Values are defined as socially defined desires and goals that are internalised through the process of conditioning, learning of socialisation and those become subjective preferences, standards and aspirations. According to Radha Kamal Mukharjee 'values reflect different philosophical positions'. Most of these are idealistic values. The concept of values is closely associated with the concept of man. Values are classified in different ways by the Eastern and Western philosophers.

Values are only vaguely or roughly understood by the Western philosophers. Schofield observes in this context that "In case education of and indeed in case of values the terms remain nebulous because we know vaguely or roughly what they mean and as a result never discipline ourselves to ask what exactly they mean". Values mean worth or importance. Value can only be thought of clearly when one thinks about the types of values. According to Western philosophers, values are commonly known as two broad typcs—Absolute and Pragmatic values. Absolute values are the contributions of idealism. They have universal validity. They represent true reality. They are not bound by time and space or other physical limitations. They may be stated to have been derived from Plato's concept of absolute ideas. Kant's philosophy contributed to the categorical imperative of 'doing good'. Schofield says, "For idealists, absolute values are the supreme authority, they represent the ultimate reality". Absolutes are thought of to be determining the behaviour of man. Hence, they determine the content of education, according to idealists.

The values of pragmatism are quite different from that of idealism. Pragmatic values are sometimes known as instrumental values too. For John Dewey, absolute ideas are not the governing factors but the personal experiences of man governing their behaviours. The experiences of the persons is quite important to him, both in morality and education. So he described education, as the "continual reconstruction of experiences". Whatever works in right, knowledge that is useful is important. Schofield says, "neither the idea of absolute values nor the idea of pragmatic values is entirely satisfactory". Perhaps a balancing position between the two has to be achieved.

According to the Indian philosophers, knowledge has two functions. Theoretical, that is revealing the existence of some object, and practical, that is helping in the fulfilment of a purpose in life. The first one is known as 'fact' and the other as 'value'. Both are interrelated because knowledge of facts leads to pursuit of a value. According to Indian philosophers, values are classified into four classes, viz., 1. Dharma (Virtue), 2. Artha (Wealth), 3. Kama (Pleasure), 4. Moksha (Self-realisation).

Values may also be classified as either intrinsic or instrumental. For example, in quenching thirst by drinking water, water is instrumental, while quenching thirst by it is intrinsic. Usually the term 'value is used for the ends sought, but the means of their attainment is also called values. Of the above values, Dharma is a moral value, Kama is a psychological value. Artha is an economic value and Moksha is a spiritual value. Dharma is a moral value spoken in case of human beings only. It is superior to the other two values of Artha and Kama. Speaking truth, kindness, purity, etc., come under Dharma. Dharma is related to Kama and Artha. Artha is a means for Kama while Dharma furnishes the necessary criteria for Kama. Dharma is regulative philosophy of life. Hence, Dharma is a means as well as an end. It is instrumental as well as intrinsic. It subserves Moksha. Moral purification helps in the conquest of lower self. Besides the above four values, this philosophy also speaks of Trinity of values— "Satyam, Shivam and Sundaram". The Western philosophers have upheld the idealistic valuation of Truth (Satyam), Goodness (Shivam) and Beauty (Sundaram). The divergence in the conceptualisation of these idealistic values has resulted to some extent in the value crisis.

Various philosophers have different stands on values. Idealism stresses on the importance of the exaltation of human personality and higher values in life. Naturalism on the other hand lacks ideals. It lays stress on individual relation and assertion against social advancement or social co-operation. Pragmatism emphasises on child's individuality, his needs, interests and aptitudes, its principles of learning by doing, activity and experience. Pragmatism is an in and out utilitarian philosophy. Each of these philosophies has something very useful and substantial to contribute to the field of education. No single philosophy is suitable and sufficient for all the times, places and people. Hence, it is essential to make an attempt to synthesise or to select and to draw together ideas and aspects from different philosophies, known as the Eclectic Tendency in education. It is also called a 'philosophy of fusion' or 'philosophy or compromise' which pieces together different beliefs in philosophy and finds harmony among the various philosophical positions and evolves a practical method of application of the finest principles needed in the educational field. An educator tries to put together and creates an educational philosophy and practice of his own to suit the contemporary environment. A close examination of various philosophies reveals that none of them provide all the answers for the ultimate questions of life. There are many rigid schools of thought, specially in India and such thoughts are not conducive to national and emotional integration. Thus, philosophies of education are complementary and not contradictory. Idealism is fundamental while naturalism and pragmatism are contributory in the theory and practice of education.

This book is an analysis of John Dewey's philosophy of education. It is proposed to identify his priorities, beliefs, convictions and experiences in matters related to the educational practices. It is assumed that his works, directly or indirectly, reveal his educational thought and philosophy and values of education which he believes.

1. The Biographical Sketch

The brief biographical sketch herein has been given to bring in a human touch and to create a rapport with the thinker, John Dewey.

2. The Philosophy of Life

A brief account of the philosophy the life of John Dewey was given to indicate the basic goal which he has and tried to achieve as this indication is likely to help to understand the essential spirit of the philosopher John Dewey.

3. The Education

Education is an essential human virtue. Without it, man is a splendid slave, a reasoning savage. It is to humanise him. Man becomes man through education. He is what education makes him. Man is an animal, both from his passions and his reason. Education fashions and models him for the society. Education has been widely discussed and interpreted by different thinkers, philosophers and educationists with reference to its aims, functions and implications. It is a historical fact that the framework of education is determined to a great extent by the sociological impact of a particular time. In this category, it was attempted to describe the concept of education according to Dewey.

4. The Aims of Education

Education, we are often told, is a system. It cannot be a haphazard undertaking. Education is a human necessity and an ornament that adorns human life. It is a living activity directed to some goal. If so, one may obviously ask, 'what is the aim' the goal or the objective of this activity? This question is bound to arise in the mind of either a lay person or even an expert in the field of education. This question becomes more urgent to be answered, clearly and precisely. Here, an attempt was made to explain the aims of education according to John Dewey.

5. The Methods of Teaching and Learning

By method it is meant that a link is developed between the students, the teacher and the subject matter. Education is a process of knowing things. It is an act of producing knowledge and an instrument of getting knowledge. Hence, education as a process actualises itself through various aids and devices which are mostly psychological in nature. Some of them are purely subjective or marked by external characteristics. These aids and devices of teaching and learning are generally known as methods of education. Different educationists and philosophers have prescribed different techniques of teaching and learning according to their bent of mind or mental disposition and scheme of education. Hence, an attempt was made to explain the methods of teaching and learning proposed by John Dewey.

6. The Teacher

In the process of education, teacher is the pivotal point, and the heart of the matter. Education takes place through the interaction between the teacher and the taught. He is the maker of man. The true textbook for the pupil is his teacher. He trains the minds, cultivates the manners and shapes the morals of the members of the community at their most impressionable age. He is to be more honoured than the parents, because, parents give children their life but the teacher teaches them the art of living well. Different philosophies of education have presented the role of a teacher in the light of their principles. It was tried to explain the opinion of John Dewey about the role of the teacher in the process of the educating children.

7. The Curriculum

The concept of curriculum being the content of education may be deemed as the practical side of philosophy. The curriculum means 'a run way' —a course which one runs to reach a goal. In this sense, education becomes a race, run on the course of curriculum, to reach the goal of full development of a child's personality. It embodies all the experiences which are utilised by the school to attain the aims of education. It is constructed in accordance with the aims of education that are ultimately guided by the objectives of life, over which, philosophy has a great bearing. In the light of different, philosophies, different types of curriculum have been presented. Here, an attempt was made to explain the curriculum proposed by John Dewey.

8. The Discipline

The nature of concept of discipline is governed by the philosophy of life. In other words, discipline reflects the philosophy of life. It reflects the philosophical pre-possessions or particular ideologies. Here, it was attempted to describe the concept of discipline given by John Dewey.

9. The Values

The East and West have contributed to the philosophy of values. The concept of values is very important in education. The concept of education is to be visualised as nothing but a set of values in essence. Education is the transmission of what is worthwhile in those who become committed to it. It was attempted to know the values suggested by John Dewey.

2

The Biography

John Dewey, the American philosopher, psychologist, practical teacher and one of the greatest thinkers of the present age, was born in 1859 and grew to manhood in Burlington, Vermont. He was nurtured as a child and youth in a nineteenth century new England town. A boy, growing up in New England experiences nature in its extremes. He and his brothers absorbed naturally the unusual beauty of the Vermont environment. Dewey's father, Archibald Dewey, made an adequate income as a store keeper and the boys helped out by carrying newspapers and tallying lumber brought down the lakes from Canada. In this pre-industrial town most of the children shared in the activities and responsibilities of the home. In the course of growing up, they became aware, at first hand, of the round of simple industrial and agricultural occupations. His mother, Lucina, was a convert to Congregationalism from a universalist background. Her emphasis was a moral judgement rather than on religious dogmatism. She read widely, had a quick inquiring mind and played an active role in the social and intellectual life of Burlington. On the whole, Dewey was brought up in a rural environment.

The young John attended traditional district schools in Burlington. Compared to the concrete learnings from family and community, work in the town seemed a bore. The schools were overcrowded and without careful regulations of attendance. They lacked a uniformity on graded courses of study and the teachers were poorly selected.

The experiences of early years brought to him two convictions (1) that traditional methods of schooling were useless and (2) that human contacts of everyday life provide unlimited, natural dynamics learning situations. He heard the lively comments and discussions in his fathers shop and realised the strength and power of group consciousness in the various activities of small society. These two convictions directed the course of his educational work.

Shortly before his 16th birthday Dewey entered the university of Vermont. He graduated from that university in 1879. He studied philosophy for another year. In that year he plunged into the study of philosophy reading and labouring far into the night. With the result he topped the class and got the highest marks on record in philosophy (Max, Easterman, Heroes I have known, 1942, p. 282).

He was confronted with a philosophical problem that preoccupied him for a life time. How to resolve the chasms that seemed to separate the material and moral sciences. At Vermont this issue was represented in the gap between the organic revolutionary view of Huxley and the dominating philosophy on campus, which Dewey described as Scottish institutionalism. The latter was as the champion of traditional morals and religion as against the skeptical tendencies in sensational empiricism.

It taught that man is born with certain ultimate and unexplainable principles which are intuitively recognised as true and which are taken for granted by common sense without any logical proof. Man is under necessity to accept them, for lacking these self evident institutions, he is without starting points for his thought and without standards for his conduct. Such intuitively known principles are to be found in grammar, logic, mathematics, aesthetics, ethics, religion and metaphysics and supply strong evidence for the existence of God, the soul, immortality freedom duty, etc.

Dewey came to see the institutionalism so typical of New England duealist heritage that he felt a need to oppose for the rest of his life. The depth of his feeling was revealed years later, when he described this tradition as representing "divisions by way of isolation of self from the world, of soul from body, of nature from God" that were felt by him as an inward laceration". The demand for a unifying philosophy to resolve these separations was experienced as an intense emotional cracking. A glimpse of such an alternative had been first suggested in his experience with Huxley. In the eighties it was to lead him to Hegel and then gradually to the elaboration of experimentalism within the evolutionary orientation.

Upon graduating from the University of Vermont in 1879 Dewey taught high school courses for two years in South Oil City, Pennsylvania, a position he obtained through his cousin, who was the principal of the school. He taught a little of everything including Latin, algebra and natural science. His duties as a beginning teacher consumed only part of his energies and the speculative quests that he had begun in Vermont occupied his attention. He read philosophy avidly far into the nights and became very absorbed.

Max Eastman reports that Dewey told him that it was during an evening in Oil City that he had a "mystic experience". It came as an answer to a question still worrying him, whether he really meant business when he prayed "It was not a dramatic mystic experience. There was not a vision, not even a definable emotion just a supremely blissful feeling that his worries were over". Dewey held that such an experience cannot be described in words, but in earthly language he tried to convey the feeling that came" what the hell are you worrying about anyway? Everything that's here is here and you can just lie back on". (Eastman, 1942). Many years later, we find Dewey returning to this theme in more elegant language, in a major statement on his religious orientation, a common faith. He referred to his faith as one of natural piety and contrasted it with what he called unreligious attitudes.

He remained as a teacher for a brief spell and then proceeded to John Hopkins University. After two years, he got his Ph.D there. Dewey got a first hand experience with a university as a centre for advancing knowledge through disciplined inquiry. That became a guiding ideal in plants for his own later work. He took a course in elocution because he was timid and unsure as a speaker. His greatest satisfaction however came from his work with George Sylboster Morris who introduced Dewey to Hegel. A close relationship grew between them.

Hegel's views of reality as an organic unity whose parts were interrelated like those of a biological organisms met Dewey's deep need for an alternative to be dualism he detested. As he himself put it "Hegel's synthesis of subject and object, matter and spirit, the divine and human operated as an immense relief, a liberation. He gets treatment of human culture, of institutions and the arts involved, the dissolution's of hard and fast dividing walls and had a special attraction for me" (Adams and Montague, 1930).

Dewey later found Hegel's schematism artificial, however, Hegel left permanent marks and it helped Dewey to begin the integration that he sought in his own thinking. This was evidenced for example, in the early forming of his social philosophy. In independent reading, he had been impressed deeply by Comte's analysis of the disorganised character of modern Western culture, due to disintegrative "individualism" and by his idea of a synthesis of science that would provide a regulative method for organised social life.

He found these criticisms in Hegel, but with a deeper, more far reaching integration. This theme was to be sounded later in individualism, old and new and in many writings on a democratic social order. Its influence was to be shown, too, in his idea that the life of the school should be conceived as an organic community. At a more general level, Dewey's tendency to define sense, so that answer would represent resolutions of apparent polar opposites reminds us of Hegel's idealistic style.

Dewey experiments in the psychological laboratory with G. Stanley Hall, one of the major minds on company, resulted in the two important influences (1) a feeling of dissatisfaction with the idealistic view of mind and (2) the feeling that a philosophically oriented rational psychology would have to give way to experiment. These ideas were to come to the surface some years later under the stimulation of reading William James.

The telling influence for Dewey's immediate career was his encounter with Hegel through his study with Morris—Dewey was now clear that his commitment was to philosophy. Finally in July, 1884, he received an offer from President James, B. Angell of the University of Michigan to become an instructor at a salary of nine hundred dollars. He remained there till 1894. Dewey affirmed that Hegellian Philosophy "in its broad and essential features is, identical with the theological teaching of Christianity". He was active in the first congregational church where he conducted Bible classes, in 1887-1888 on "Church History". Later his ethical interest shifted from religious to a social orientation. But his concern with the ethical dimension was constant throughout his career.

It was during the latter part of his stay at Michigan that Dewey began to move away from Hegelianism. The growing commitment to a functionally oriented psychology with its roots in evolutionary biology was a leading factor in this shift. James principles of psychology exerted a critical influence in leading Dewey to assign major significance to the idea of total organisms interacting with its environment and actively engaged in adjusting to it. James, thought, life in terms of action. He conceived of mind not as something apart from nature, but as the process by which organisms and environment become integrated. The objective conception of mind Dewey said work its way more and more into all my ideas and acted as a ferment to transform old beliefs" (Adams Montague, p. 24).

Dewey's interest in primary and secondary education began while he was at Michigan. He became aware that the quality of the secondary school was dependent on the training the child had received in the grade schools. This lead him to study programmes of elementary schools. He became convinced that work there did not coincide with the normal learning process of young children. He came to attribute the shortcomings of the school to all concerned programmes and methods and to poor co-ordination of the various levels. Thus he began his search for an alternative that would integrate educational, psychological and philosophical ideas.

Within a few years the quest was to culminate in the founding of the laboratory school at the University of Chicago. The Michigan phase should not be passed off without the mention of another factor that also turned his interests to education.

In 1886, Dewey married Alice Chipman, a young woman who had a deep interest in philosophy. She was a Charter Member of the Philosophical Society and took most of the work offered by the department. Her vigorous independent mind and strong interests in social issues were to act as an intellectual stimulant to her husband's thought. In 1894, he was appointed head of the Department of Philosophy in the University of Chicago. From 1902 to 1904, he was also the Director of Schools of Education. In 1896, he founded his "Laboratory school" in the university which brought him world fame. All his theories were tested in this school. His concepts of education were modified and clarified in the light of practical experience of the school situation. In 1904, he was appointed as professor of philosophy at the University of Columbia and held this post upto 1930. Afterwards, he remained there Professor Emeritus, until he died in 1952. During these years, he undertook educational engagements and commissions abroad. He visited countries like Japan, China, Turkey, Russia, etc. In 1919, he lectured on philosophy of education at the University of Tokyo and then spent two years at the University of Peking. In the thirties, he was invited by the Turkish government to suggest the reorganisation of the Turkish Schools. He so influenced the course of education in these countries that schools were reorganised on the lines suggested by him.

Dewey's Writings

Dr. Dewey as a prolific writer. A large number of volumes and hundred of articles came from his pondering his sixty years of life as an educationist. Many of his publications had to do with pure philosophy and are of interest to students who wish to acquire a more accurate knowledge of his fundamental theories.

The chief works on education by John Dewey are:

1896 — Interests and Efforts as Related to Will

1899 — The Schools and Society

1902	—	The Child and the Curriculum
1910	—	How We Think?
1913	—	Interest and Effort in Education
1915	—	Schools of Tomorrow (with Evelyn Dewey)
1916	—	Democracy and Education
1920	—	Reconstruction in Philosophy
1922	—	Human Nature and Conduct. An Introduction to Social Psychology
1925	—	Experience and Nature
1929	—	The Quest for Certainty. A Study of the Relation of Knowledge and Action
1929	—	Sources of a Science of Education

3

The Philosophy of Life

For those who believe it is the philosophers task to juggle the universe on the point of an argument, Dewey is a complete disappointment. The world he starts out and also ends with is the common world we all live in and experience everyday of our lives.

Deweys philosophy and programme have been variously termed as "Experimentalism' 'Functionalism' 'Progressivism' 'Practicalism' and above all 'Pragmatism'. All these indicate his emphasis on the dynamic and ever-changing character of life.

John Dewey is the most important single force in the progressive education movement. Building on various sporadic reforms that had been initiated, he developed a new philosophy of learning and logic of thinking and laid down the comprehensive philosophic foundations that made it possible for the new education to develop and prosper.

The main ingredients of Dewey's philosophy are:

1. Truth is that which works, which fulfils our purposes.
2. There are no fixed values. All values change with time and space. Man's life is a series of experiments and purposeful actions.

3. Everything is provisional. Nothing is ultimate. Knowledge is a means and never an end in itself.
4. Knowledge and thinking are associated with action. Action is superior to thought but at the same time thought and action are complementary.

In the beginning Dewey was immensely influenced by Hegel the idealist. But gradually he was drawn towards the ideas of William James and Charles Pierce and ultimately he became a confirmed advocate of pragmatism. His chief importance lies in his criticism of the traditional notion of truth, which is embodied in the theory that he calls intutionalism. According to Dewey the function of philosophy is not to know the world, but to control and improve it. According to this approach the function of philosophy is concerned with the study of those social problems and intricacies that arise because of interaction between democracy, industry and science. Due to the feature of philosophy its method becomes experimental and the principal objective of the method is to find out solutions of social and moral problems of man.

Dewey's, philosophy is fundamentally, derivative from his analysis of scientific method. According to him, philosophy to be significant and intelligent, must be scientific, that is must follow in its inquiries the method of science. Deweys whole philosophic effort is concerned with doing for our epoch what the classicals did for theirs. Just as they took their science as exemplar of what knowledge is and the method of their science as standard method of knowing, Dewey takes modern science as example of what knowledge is and the method of modern science as standard of the method of knowing.

Dewey turned exclusively towards the natural science and he proclaimed his adherence to Watson behaviourism. For Dewey there is no real knowledge other than the knowledge gained by the methods of natural science. The natural inclination of every modern scientist is to be Aristotelian. Dewey was also an Aristotelian. His doctrine was that knowledge is an exemplification of one of the ways of nature. His doctrine, that all knowledge must have passed experimental test before it can be considered knowledge are sufficient proofs of the general statement.

Experimentalism is one of the two basic terms Dewey used to designate his philosophy. The other is instrumentalism. The basic of Dewey's constructive philosophy is his analysis and evaluation of experiment. The primary designation of Dewey's whole philosophy is experimentalism because its foundation is his philosophy of experiment. The method of experimentation is the very essence of the method of modern science, it is the flesh and blood (not the bone) over which Dewey's whole philosophy stands. Grant that dewey's analysis of scientific experimentation is in its principal contentions sound and valid and one will have to grant that pretty much everything else fundamental in his philosophy is sound and valid. (Deny the general validity of his claim concerning the place and function of experimentation in scientific method and then, no matter how much else of his philosophy you may like and accept, it will be a liking and accepting theses and thats'). Thus Dewey does not substantially tear out experimental practice from scientific inquiry.

To understand anything of his philosophy then it is essential to understand Dewey's conception of science. It is not an extremely complicated idea, although he often referred to it as being highly theoretical. This tendency in the human organism is fundamental. Dewey was greatly influenced by this point of view. He took this simple idea with its essential aspects and developed it consistently so that it served as the basis of theories in all phases of philosophy of education. The key notions in Dewey's idea of the scientific method of thinking, are control, experiment and objective test. His aim reiterated constantly, is to bring the scientific method of reflective thought to all phases of human activity, including politics, art and morals.

It was not only the actual content and method of science that interested, and indeed preoccupied Dewey, but the connotations that were associated with science objectivity, honesty, freedom and open mindedness. According to him, philosophy was to follow the spirit of science, not only in its approach to problems of metaphysics and epistemology, but also in the fields of ethics and aesthetics. Dewey saw democracy as the political manifestation of scientific method, with its combination of purposiveness and objectivity, freedom and discipline, individual speculation and public verification. Democracy and science came closest to being the only absolutes in Deweys experimentalist philosophy.

Dewey does not consider any object of idea permanent. He believed in social change. Since social change is inevitable, the social and moral problems of society always change. Therefore, the assumption of definiteness of anything, idea is doubtful. He does not believe in any divine power. He has strong faith in the power of man. He says that man will have to make his own effort for his development and progress. So man will have to depend on his creative intelligence.

Dewey does not see any difference between knowledge and experience. According to him knowledge is only a result of our various types of experiences. He does not believe in any pre-determined truth. He does not accept the permanence of truth of reality forever.

The important contributions Dewey has made, which entitle him to be enrolled among the great philosophers of modern times, are not to metaphysics but to the other fields of philosophy. "Though his proposals for the reform of education, his illuminating analysis of the process of logic and reflective thinking, his clarification of the ideals of democracy, his insistence that art should be integrated with living and his courageous facing of the difficulties of the present era, untrammelled by the inertia of customs and traditions, he was introduced a new spirit into the modern philosophy which is invaluable" (Wright, William Kelley, A History of Modern Philosophy, p. 558).

4

The Education

Speaking generally, education signifies the sum total of processes of by which a community or social group, whether small or large, transmits its acquired power and aims with a view to securing it's own continued existence and growth's —Dewey. The most notable distinction between living and inanimate things is that the former maintain themselves by renewal. It is the very nature of life to strive to continue in being. Since this continuance can be secured only by constant renewals, life is a self renewing process. With nutrition and production are to physiological life education is to social life. The education, consists primarily in transmission through communication. Communication is a process of sharing experience till it becomes a common possession.

Education is the development of all those capacities in the individual which will enable him to control his environment and fulfil his responsibilities. The educational doctrines of Dewey are chiefly rooted in psychology. Emphasising the social aspects of education, he approached its problems psychologically. Education has always occupied the central place in Dewey's philosophy of Democracy.

"Education is the fundamental of social progress and reform". All education proceeds by the participation of the individual in the social consciousness of the race". Education according to Deway is a necessity of life or a social necessity. "The function of education is to help the growing of a helpless young animal into a happy, moral and efficient human being" accounts the main function of education in equipping the child in the art of successful living (Dewey, My Pedagogic Creed).

Each phase of a growing life has it's own distinctive needs, qualities and powers. The process of education for each phase must be such that the needs of the individual are satisfied, his qualities are enriched and the powers are matured (Dewey, My Pedagogic Creed).

Participation in collective activities creates social environment and gives knowledge of sociability. Collective work enables the child to understand the aim and purpose of work and gives him necessary method and ability to do that work. Education is a process of living and not a preparation for future living—For Dewey, education is not a preparation for life. It is life or growth. Education should make man social and worthy of the society. (Dewey, My Pedagogic Creed).

According to Dewey "True education comes through the stimulation of the child's powers by the demands of social situations in which he finds himself". The basis of all education is the interests of the child and those of the society. He says, "The purpose of education is to give the young the things they need in order to develop in an orderly, sequential way into members of the society" (Dewey, Education Today).

According to him education is a bipolar process. One is psychological and the other is sociological, neither of which can be subordinated or neglected. "Education must begin with a psychological insight in the child's capacities, interests and habits". (Dewey, My Pedagogic Creed).

The child instincts and inclinations should necessarily be studied. These should be brought into exercise in the social situations. These should be translated into their social equivalents.

The psychological side of the child is the starting point of all education. Without an insight into the psychological structure and the activities of the individual, the educative process will be haphazard and arbitrary. The main purpose of education is to create harmony between the individual and social development. Social outlook means creation of useful environment which is in concurrence with social conditions.

"Every worthwhile education is a direct enrichment of the life of the young and not merely a more or less repellent preparation for the duties of adult life" (Dewey, Education Today).

Dewey emphasised experience, experiment, purposeful leaving, freedom and other well known concepts of progressive education. He interprets education "as the scientific method by means of which man studies the world, acquires cumulatively knowledge of meanings and values". Education in order to accomplish its ends, both for the individual learners and for the society must be based upon existence (Dewey, Experience and Education).

According to Dewey every experience should do something to prepare a person for later experiences of a deeper and more expansive quality. That is the very meaning of growth, continuity, reconstruction of experience. A fully integrated personality, on the other hand, exists only when successive experiences are integrated with one another, Dewey emphasised on learning by doing. He gave much importance to activity. According to him knowledge is derived from activity. Knowledge and action being intimately connected, can't stand apart from one another moreover, while action gives birth to knowledge, modifies further action Dewey advocated life centred education and announced that education could be integrated with life only by organising education around adult occupations (Education from Dewey to Gandhi, 1962).

'Education is a development within, by, and for experience'. Education is a process of reconstruction of experience, giving it a more socialised value through the medium of increased social efficiency. The principle that development of experience comes about through interaction means that education is essentially a social process.

The principle of interaction makes it clear that failure of adoption of material to needs and capacities of individuals may cause an experience to be non-educative. The principle of continuity in its educational means, nevertheless, that the future has to be taken into account at every stage of the educational process (Dewey, Experience and Education).

"There is, I think, no point in the philosophy of progressive education, which is sounder than its emphasis upon the importance of the participation of the learner in the formation of the purposes which direct his activities in the learning process. Children are individuals whose freedom should be respected. The new education emphasises the freedom of the learner" (Dewey, Experience and Education).

According to Dewey the child is born with certain powers and capacities. Those powers are to be dèveloped according to the demands of the society. So education should enable the individual child to act and react with his environment to gain experience for proper social adjustment.

It is a sound educational principle that students should be introduced to scientific subject matter and be initiated into its facts and laws through acquaintance with every day social applications. According to Dewey, "True education comes through the stimulation of the child's powers by the demands of social situations in which he finds himself". The basis of all education is the interests of the child and those of the society.

5

The Aims of Education

Dewey, being a pragmatic educator, contends that there are no fixed and ultimate aims of education. Aims are proximate. The aims grow out of the existing situations. It is not to reach at any prefixed final goal. Education therefore, is a means as well as an end. According to Dewey there are four functions of education.

Education is a Process of Growth

His words are—growth, unlimited and illimitable. Thus, growth must be wise and economical and directed towards a desirable end. The aim of education is more education and the end of growth is more growth. What the child learns in the class is growing. In the words of Dewey, "The process of education is a continuous process of adjustment, having as its aim at every stage an added capacity of growth (Dewey—How we think, p. 61).

Education is Life and Life is Education

Dewey says that life is a by-product of activities and education is born out of these activities. He rejected the idea that education is preparation for life. If at all it is preparation for life then it is preparation through life experiences. The child lives in the present. The future is meaningless to him. Hence, it is absurd to require him to do things for some future preparation. School being an extension of home, provides life experiences to the child.

Education Leads Towards Social Efficiency

Dewey says "What nutrition and reproduction are to physiological life, education is to social life". Man is essentially a social being, a citizen, growing and thinking in a vast complex of interactions and relations. Though education, he is developing reasoning in social relations, cultivating social virtues and thus becoming socially efficient. At the same time he is developing social awareness and social sensitiveness. Social efficiency includes economic and cultural efficiency. The term given by Dewey in this regard is "Socialisation of an individual".

Experience is the Basis of his Philosophy

Dewey says that education is "the process of the reconstruction or reconstitution of experience, giving it a more socialised value through the medium of increased individual efficiency". Every generation inherits experiences from its past generation and these experiences are modified according to the developing situations. With their own experiences and participation, individuals reconstruct new experiences suiting the changing circumstances and problems of life. The individual has to face old as well as new situations and problems from time to time. Hence, his activities should also be changing accordingly. Thus, experience is serviced or re-organised. This is a continuous process. The role of education is to create conditions for promotion of continuity of experiences.

John Dewey, a true pragmatic educator has no fixed aims of education. He believes that since physical and social environments are always changing, aims of education must also change. They cannot be fixed for all times to come. Thus, he revolted against the traditional aims of education, namely the moral aim; the disciplinary aim and the knowledge aim etc. of the 19th century. He rejected the very idea of education as preparation for future life and said that education must cater to the present needs of the child rather than the future because the child is not interested in the unknown future. He, therefore, said that educational aims must be restated and reformulated in the light of the rapid social and economic changes in every day life.

According to Dewey, an aim denotes the result of any natural process brought to consciousness and made a factor in determining present observation and choice of ways of acting. It signifies that an activity has become intelligent. Specifically it means foresight of the alternative consequences attendant upon acting in a given situation in different ways, and the use of what is anticipated to direct observation and experiment. A true aim is thus opposed at every point to an aim which is imposed upon a process of action from without. The latter is fixed and rigid, it is not a stimulus to intelligence in the given situation, but is an externally dictated order to do such and such things. Instead of connecting directly with present activities it is remote, divorced from the means by which it is to be reached. Instead of suggesting a free and better-balanced activity it is a limit set of activity. In education, the currency of these externally imposed aims is responsible for the emphasis put upon the notion preparation for a remote future and for rendering the work of both teacher and pupil mechanical and slavish.

As such John Dewey does not believe in any ultimate aim of education. In his Democracy and Education, writing on education he says, 'It has all time an immediate end, and so far as activity is educative it reaches that end, the direct transformation of the quality of experience. Infancy, youth, adult life, all stand on the same educative level in the sense that what is really learned at any and every stage of experience constitutes the value of the experience...". Thus Dewey finds the aim of education in the process itself. The aim of education is not to reach any prefixed final goal. Aim is the immediate end catching attention. Education is to remake experience. As Dewey says "The process of education is a continuous process of adjustment, having its aim at every stage and added capacity of growth". The individual has always to readjust himself to the environment. As long as this process of readjustment is continued education goes on. Since this readjustment never stops and the individual is always in the process of learning things, education never stops in life. Evidently, no such final foal or end of education can be conceived at which education is to be completed. Furthermore, the aim of education is not to be determined by the educator. It is the child himself who has to choose his own aim.

Dewey attack the type of education which attempted to train the individual for specific adult life. He agreed to the function as preparation for life, if it refers to life now and the immediate future. The fostering of continuous healthy growth ensured adequate preparation for immediate life. Dewey also agreed with the aim of education as 'self-realisation of the individual' if the teacher looks into the distant imaginary product, but to the present and at a pupil who exists, who grows, develops and achieves realisation of all his powers all the time. It is in the active development of the pupil that Dewey sees the place for individual education and the education of individuality. He wants each pupil's power and personality to be developed not according to any absolute standard but according to pupil's own capacities and opportunities. The pupil's progress is to be measured by his own best standard and should not be set against those of the other pupils who differ in natural ability, environmental experience and temperament. It is the duty of the teacher to observe individual desire and behaviour and should seek these tendencies to strength the process of growth. Education he says protects, sustains and directs growth. Similarly Dewey would attempt cultural aims is one of the aims of education. So long as it allows refining and guiding of personal tastes rather than an imposition of arbitrary standard (V.R. Taneja, 1983).

Thus, the important function and aim of education is to create a social environment in which the child may successfully participate for social awakening of mankind.

The education should enable man to understand his past as well as future experiences. Education should create such a capacity in the child that he is able to face social situations strongly and come out successfully in the struggle, only that education is useful which creates the will to develop continuously. Education gives man such an insight that he is able to gather necessary means.

In a recent publication Deweys theory has been analysed into four key propositions.

1. The aim of education should be to reach the child to think not what to think.
2. Education should be for both hands and minds of the children.
3. Life only educates.
4. The school now divorced from life, must be reunited with it through activities that will simplify its relationships, develop it's essential meaning, eliminate it's unworthy and obsolescent features and extend the individual social environment (Charles, W., Cutler and Richard S. Rimanoczy, A. Layman's guide to Education).

Certain common principles aimed by progressive schools are:

1. Expression and cultivation of individuality;
2. Learning through experience;
3. Free activity;
4. Acquisition of skills and techniques as means of attaining ends which make direct vital appeal;
5. Making the most of the opportunities of present life;
6. Acquaintance with a changing world (Dewey, Experience and Education, pp. 5-6).

6

The Methods of Teaching and Learning

Method is a statement of the way the subject matter of an experience develops most effectively and fruitfully. It is derived, accordingly, from observation of the course of experiences where there is no conscious distinction of personal attitude and the manner from material dealt with. The assumption that method is something separate, is connected with the notion of the isolation of mind and self from the world of things. It makes instruction and learning, formal, mechanical and constrained. While methods are individualised, certain features of the normal course of an experience to it's fruition may be discriminated, because of general similarities in the material dealt with, from time to time. Expressed in terms of the attitude of the individual the traits of a good method are straight forwardness, flexible, intellectual, interest or open minded will to learn, integrity of purpose and acceptance of responsibility for the consequences of one's activity including thought.

Dewey is quite against the traditional methods of teaching. He emphasises direct experience as the basis of all methods. To him knowledge should arise from concrete and meaningful situations. Spontaneous activities should provide the natural condition for the growth of knowledge for a learner. Learning should be the result of doing. Nothing should be learned directly for its own sake. "All learning must come as a by-product of actions and never as something learned directly for it's own sake".

Concrete and meaningful situations should provide knowledge to the learner. Learning, if it is to be moral and sound, must come as a result of the normal experiences of the child. Dewey considers the mind as a product of activity and develops through activity. There must be some stimulus to mind for thinking. Mind cannot think unless it is faced with some problem. As soon as it face to face with a problem it starts thinking for it's solution. This very process Dewey applied to education. In his 'ideal school', the child engages himself in various types of activities which are inspired by his own urges and inclinations. During the course of these activities, he faces certain problems which arise freely and spontaneously out of his own life situations. The child then thinks of possible solutions and then tries to put his plans into action. In the actual execution of his plans, he comes to know of the correctness or otherwise of this idea. This he called the project method or the experimental method. With this method, Dewey emphasised the doctrine of natural interest and effort motivation.

Dewey believes that all true effort comes from a deep and natural interest in the task. If such an interest is absent, it is necessary to arouse it, because an artificial kindling of interest will be functionally bad. Dewey has declared that all learning which results from artificial stimulation is morally wrong. Hence Dewey's doctrine of natural interest effort and motivation.

Dewey advocated a number of methods of teaching and learning. Dewey recommended projects to be used as teaching techniques. This method lays emphasis on pupils' purpose, needs, interest self activity and participation in the entire process of teaching. A project is a purposeful activity proceeding in a social environment. Dewey also suggested that problematic situations should be provided to children in the classroom as well as outside the classroom. Projects or problems should not be too ambitious and beyond the pupil's capacity to accomplish.

Project Method

Dewey suggested the following steps in the project-method:

1. Creation of a suitable which gives rise to a real life problem.
2. Thinking of all possible solutions for that problem.
3. Collection of information from all possible sources.
4. Execution and arriving at the possible solution; and
5. Application of the solution arrived at.

It will thus be clear that Project Method is a democratic way of learning in which cooperation and citizenship are fostered. This method stresses on self-effort in place of memorising. Moreover, there is also correlation of activities and subjects. Since activities centre round real life problems, this procedure gives interest to pupils and appeals to them.

All learning must come as the product of experimentation. Dewey started his experimental school known as laboratory school. He wanted to test everything.

His experimental method is in tune with heuristic method.

Direct experience is the surest basis of all methods of instruction. The main function of the school is to provide an environment and improvise activities for learning through the use of their senses. It is believed that learning can be effective when it is based in the interest of the children. Interest can be aroused when children are provided activities, which have a genuine appeal for them". Once children get interested in activities, they pursue them whole heartedly, so that there is acquisition of necessary knowledge and skills". Dewey emphasised self education, self learning, play-way technique and motivation. The value of all his methods of teaching has been widely recognised. His main emphasis was the creation of suitable problematic situations and then to find the solution. This will ensure active participation of children and result in effective learning, independent thinking, originality, initiative and widening of mental horizon.

With unsurpassed clarity Dewey analysed the ills of the existing educational system. He emphasised the importance of viewing the educative process against the background of social life and he may be rightly called the exponent of social aims in education. What agitated him most was the divorce between education and life, the mutual exclusiveness between the school and the home of the child. School life, in his view was enveloped in an artificial atmosphere dominated by book learning, which stunted the growth of children. According to Dewey, such an atmosphere, produced just those tensions, which in the industrial sector, made their appearance when factory labour became the repeated performance of an assigned task whose purpose and meaning were unknown to the worker. He drew the attention of the public, to the urgent need to stop the rote and integrate the school with the society, and the curriculum with home life, so that the student might, in after years, meet the challenge, of the gathering tensions in the social structure. He condemned the undue importance given to book learning and said that learning should come through activities. The activities, in order to be capable of leading the child to learning, should be related to the actual life of the child. For this purpose he advocated the introduction of adult occupations as the core round which the entire curriculum should be built.

The school life of the child should be an indistinguishable part of its normal life while the previous epoch emphasised the inclinations of the child as the basis of educational methodology, Dewey took his stand on the needs of the child as real living member of the society, not merely as a novitiate for life. This pattern of education may be called life centred education. "Each phase of growing, life has it's own distinctive needs, qualities and powers. The organisation of study and the methods of teaching must, for each phase be such that the process of learning will satisfy the needs, enrich the qualities and motive the powers of the individual" (Dewey, Education Today).

Dewey advocated the use of natural activities as the basis of teaching and learning". Dewey believes that all education proceeds by the participation of the individual in the social consciousness of the race. This process begins unconsciously almost at birth and is continually shaping the individuals powers, saturating his consciousness forming his habits, training his ideas and arousing his feelings and emotions through his unconscious education. The individual gradually comes to share in the intellectual and moral resources which humanity has succeeded in getting together. He becomes an inheritor of the funded capital of civilization. The most formal and technical education in the world cannot safely depart from this general process. It can only organise it or differentiate it in some particular direction (Dewey, My Pedagogic Creed).

To 'Learn from Experience' is to make a backward and forward connection between what we do to things and what we enjoy (or) suffer from things in consequence. Under such conditions, doing becomes a trying, an experiment with the world to find out what it is like, the undergoing becomes instruction—discovery of the connection of things (Dewey, Democracy and Education).

The continuous enrichment of experience by readjusting to the complexities of the environment constitutes therefore, the heart of education. He emphasised "Learning through experience and acquisition of isolated skills and techniques as a means of attaining ends which make direct vital appeal" (Dewey, Experience and Education).

The method of teaching is the method of an art of action intelligently directed by ends. Method is a statement of the way the subject matter of an experience develops most effectively and fruitfully (John Dewey on Education, Selected Writings, 1964).

John Dewey follows the method 'Learning by doing' which may be called the most general method of educational pragmatism, whereby the student is put into situations with which he has to grapple. It also provides him, at the same time, with the means of dealing with them successfully. When the students learn by doing foresight, self-reliance and originality develop in them (Education, It's History and Philosophy, 1970, p. 332).

There is in Dewey analysis nothing more than the well-known method of reasoning according to inductive logic. In involves recognising a problem analysing its elements, framing a hypothesis, testing out the hypothesis, and the continuation of the process till a solution is found. This in other words is the method of experimentalism. Experimentalism method means that we have no right to call anything knowledge except where our activity actually produced certain physical changes in things, which agree with and confirm the conception entertained. Short of such specific changes, our beliefs are only hypothesis, suggestions, guesses are to be entertained, tentatively and to be utilised as indications of experiments to be tried. (Dewey, Democracy and Education).

The application of the principle of the experimental method is quite old and comes from the doctrine of the useful, as advocated by Bacon Locker, Roussean and others. But Dewey deserves credit for making educators fully aware of the significance of the process in the development of the mind. This principle has formed the basis for his insistence upon methods of instruction that are in accord with the normal course of mental activity. From this analysis of how the mind works there have come into recent methodology the so-called functional method, project method, problem method and the activity programme.

Dewey's methods of teaching comprised three processes.

1. Continuance of psychological order in the curriculum.
2. Retention of problem method.
3. Extension of social opportunity.

The first is natural and therefore essential. The second would enable the pupils to learn 'not things but the meaning of things'. Social opportunities would arouse social consciousness an essential factor for future citizens. (V.R. Taneja, 1983).

Project method is the practical outcome of Dewey's philosophy. It is employed by educationists all over the world. The method translates the idea of education through occupations into a form suitable for the ordinary school. Instead of learning lessons from the teacher, the pupils are faced with some task to be solved. If the project is suited to the age and experience of the children, the interest it created carried them beyond the immediate activity into varied learning. (V.R. Taneja, 1983).

According to Dewey the active side precedes the passive in the development of the child—nature, that expression comes before conscious impression, that the muscular development precedes the sensory, that movements come before conscious sensations. Consciousness is essentially motor or impulsive, that conscious states tend to project themselves in action.

— Ideas (intellectual and rational processes) result from action. As a result we present the child with arbitrary symbols. Symbols are a necessity in mental development, but they have their place, as tools for economising effort.

— The image is the great instrument of instruction. What a child gets out of any subject presented to him is simply the images which he himself forms with regard to it.

— Interests are the signs and symptoms of growing power. Accordingly the constant and careful observation of interests is the utmost importance for the educator.

— The emotions are the reflexes of actions.

Expressed in terms of the attitude of the individual, the traits of a good method are—straight forwardness, flexible intellectual interest or open minded will to learn, integrity of purpose and acceptance of responsibility for the consequences of one's activity including thought.

Activity Method

None of the method educators except Rousseau had been more insistent than Dewey, upon direct experience. However it is not so much the objects that he valued as he did the concrete and meaningful situations. In as much as learning comes indirectly in response to action, the situations which arouse activities furnish the natural condition for the growth of knowledge. Emphasising the point of view Dewey says.

"The first approach to any subject in school, if thought is to be aroused and not words acquired should be as unscholastic as possible. To realise what an experience or empherical situation means, we have to call to mind the sort of situation that presents itself outside the school. The sort of occupations that interest and engage activity in ordinary life. And careful inspection of methods which are permanently successful informal education, whether in arithmetic or learning to read or studying geography or learning physics or a foreign language, will reveal that they depend for their efficiency upon the fact that they go back to the type of situation which causes reflection out of school in ordinary life. They give the pupil something to do, no something to learn, and the doing it, of such nature as to demand thinking or the intentional noting of connections, learning naturally results" (Dewey, Democracy and Education).

In the teaching process, it is to be kept in mind that the knowledge of subjects is given through natural activities. The subjects too should be correlated. Dewey wants that every subject should be correlated with the natural activities of the child, such as spinning, weaving, cooking, carpentry, leather work etc. So, Dewey gave importance to such activities in his experimental school. These activities are natural and may serve as vocational basis for the child. According to Dewey, even teaching method becomes easy through this medium. Education must begin with a physiological insight is the childs capacities, interests and habits (Dewey, My Pedagogic Creed).

Dewey emphasised the concept of purposeful learning. "There is, I think, no point in the philosophy of progressive education which is sounder than its emphasis upon the importance of the participation of the learner in the formation of the learning process" (Dewey, Experience and Education).

"The formation of purpose is, then, a rather complex intellectual operation. It involves in observation of the surrounding conditions. Knowledge of what has happened in similar situations in the past knowledge obtained partly by recollection and partly from the information, advice and warning of those who have had a wider experience. Judgement which puts together what is observed and what is recalled to see that they signify" (Dewey, Experience and Education).

Dewey proposed that the new subjects should be taught by applying them to the following teaching methods.

1. "The human mind does not learn in a vacuum. The facts presented for learning, to be grasped, must have some relation to the previous experience of the individual or to his present needs. Learning proceeds from the concrete to the general, not from the general to the particular.

2. Every individual is a little different from every other individual, not only in his general capacity and character, the differences extent, to rather minute abilities and characteristics and no amount of discipline will eradicate them. The obvious conclusion of this is that uniform methods can not possibly produce uniform results in education, that, the more we wish to come to making every one alike the more varied and individualised must the methods be.

3. Individual effort is impossible without individual interest. There can be no such things as a subject which in and by itself will furnish training for every mind. If work is not in itself interesting to the individual or does not have associations or by-products which make its doing interesting, the individual cannot put his best efforts into it, however hard one may work at it, the effort does not go into the accomplishment of work, but is largely dissipated in a moral and emotional struggle to keep the attention where it is not held" (Dewey, Education Today, p. 275).

7

The Teacher

"Teaching may be compared to selling commodities. No one can sell unless some one buys... The initiative lies with the learner, the teacher is a guide and director".

In Dewey's ideal school, the teacher occupies an important place. He is neither a lecturer nor a policeman, but a friend, guide and planner of activities. He plans activities and projects for each child on the basis of his own judgement. Then he supervises and directs, engaged in those purposeful and educative activities with a view to secure the best of growth and development, in a congenial atmosphere. The teacher in Dewey's school enjoys sufficient freedom in formulating the aims of education, in making the syllabus of studies and in devising the methods of teaching. But he is not to impose his will or authority on the pupils. He is simply to plan the environment and to guide the pupil's experience through it.

Dewey himself was a practical teacher. He was a teacher of great repute. He assigns a very important and responsible job to the teacher. The teacher has to guide the young through complexities of life. The teacher has to observe, plan and encourage pupils activities, environment and experiences. The teacher has to guide the young not only in the habit of democratic cooperation but also towards the highest intellectual pursuits and the fullest aesthetic experience. A teacher must be a professionally trained, resourceful, efficient person with sympathy for the child.

The teacher is one of the most highly productive workers. The best interests of the schools and of the people demand an intimate contact and an effective cooperation between the teachers and the others workers of the community upon whom the future of democracy depends" (Dewey, Education Today, p. 307).

Dewey gave a very important role to the teacher. "Freedom of teachers is a necessary condition of freedom for students to learn" (Dewey, Education Today). A Dewey teacher should be concerned more with his pupils impulses and interests rather than the inculcation of knowledge. "The knowledge and skill of mature person has no directive value for the experience of the immature" (Dewey, Experience and Education).

The teacher is a guide and director, he steers the boat but the energy that propels it must come from those who are learning". Dewey (Aggarwal, 1967).

"Progressive education is in connection with human experiences. Every experience is a moving force. Its value can be judged only on the ground of what it moves toward and into". The greater maturity of experience which should belong to the adult as educator puts him in a position to evaluate such experience of the young in a way the one having the less mature experience can not do. It is then the business of the educator to see in what direction an experience is heading" (Dewey, Experience and Education).

He may not have the plasticity to adopt his own personality to new growth, but teacher is ahead of his pupils in experience, he should survey the social heritage and look to a more distant purpose than his pupils. He should make a more reliable hypothesis as to the best course of action to pursue because he has more experience of life.

"The educator by the very nature of his work is obliged to see his present work in terms of what it accomplishes or fails to accomplish, for a future, whose objects are linked with those of the present". (Dewey, Experience and Education).

Competence of teachers should be judged by their skill in judging 'what will work'. The judge of this skill would be the society, which would see the quality of the product that the teacher gives to it.

The teacher, therefore, should realise his own power and responsibility to guide the young for the acquirement of the skill and his own superiority in experience and knowledge should enable the pupils to reach a stage higher than his own in the evolutionary scale. The teacher, must at the same time ensure that the individual and the group move in harmony, 'both acquiring the best and most positive habits of growth".

"The teacher business is to see that the occasion is taken advantage of since freedom resides in the operations of intelligent observation and judgement by which a purpose is developed. Guidance give by the teacher to the exercise of the pupils intelligence is an aid to freedom, not a restriction upon it. (Dewey, Experience and Education).

Instead of wasting his time in 'chalk and talk' instruction and in the establishment of rigid discipline, the teacher must observe, plan and encourage. Self discipline and group discussion develop through the will of the pupils themselves. But that does not mean that Deweyean teacher is merely to follow the child wherever he leads. Professor Dewey's child centred curriculum gave to teacher a heavier responsibility and a greater opportunity for guiding the young not only into the habit of democratic cooperation but also towards the highest intellectual pursuits and the fullest aesthetic experiences.

"Teacher should be intelligently aware of the capacities, needs and past experiences of those under instruction and secondly, should allow the suggestion made to develop into a plan and project by means of the further suggestions contribute and organised into a whole by the members of the group" (Dewey, Experience and Education).

"The more a teacher is aware of the past experiences of students, of their hopes, desires, chief interests, the better will be the understanding of the forces at work that need to be directed and utilised for the formation of reflective habits". (Dewey, How We Think). While Dewey prescribed wider range of experiences for the child, he was conscious of the danger of fruitless repetition in some cases. He therefore wanted his teacher to indicate short cuts and to persuade the pupil to engage in progressiveness activities. For this he must know the intelligence and temperament of each pupil.

The individual interests of children are not similar, they are different. The teacher should understand the individual differences in the children. This is Dewey's psychological viewpoint. If in a school, children are given opportunities of working according to their aptitudes and interests, there will be no problem of discipline. Dewey does not want any sort of autocracy in the school. Children will themselves develop morally in a social environment through natural activities.

"A primary responsibility of educators is that they not only be aware of the general principle of the shaping of actual experience by environing conditions, but that they also recognise in the concrete, what surroundings are conducive to having experiences that lead to growth. Above all, they should know how to utilise the surrounding, physical and social, that exist so as to extract from them all that they have to contribute to building up experiences that are worth while".

"The teacher should become intimately acquainted with the conditions of the social community, physical, historical, economic, occupations etc., in order to utilise them as educational resources". (Dewey, Experience and Education).

"The Teacher is engaged, not simply in the training of individuals, but in the formation of proper social life". "Every teacher should realise the dignity of his calling, that is a social servant set apart for the maintenance of proper social order and the securing of the right social growth". "In this way the teacher always is the prophet of the true God and the usherer in of the true kingdom of God". (Dewey, My Pedagogic Creed, p. 9.17).

The teacher should not consider himself superior to the child, should not give any sermons, instead should only supervise the work of the child. He is not to instruct. He is only a guide and supervisor. The teacher should stimulate the natural aptitudes of the child and should channelise them in a useful work.

According to Dewey, the development of the child should be according to the social environment. The teacher must be familiar with the social situation. It would enable him to interpret properly, the child's activities and transfer them into social channels. Education should proceed by the participation of the individual in social relationships with his fellow human beings. Acquaintance with social institutions and industrial processes takes place by actual living and working. The school is a social environment, "Simplified, purified, balanced and graded". "Originality and initiative should be the chief virtues of the school life and then learning takes place".

In the shared life, the teacher is a directing force and organiser of the environments, the best moral training is received not in the form of dictates or discipline from the teacher but as the child is directed to meet the situations arising out of the social relationships with others in the school. The teacher therefore, should not impose rules or try to form rigid habits in the child. He should select the proper influences for the child and assists him in responding to them.

"The teacher should select those things within the range of existing experience that have the promise and potentially of presenting new problems which by stimulating new ways of observations and judgement will expand the area of further experience".

"He must be aware of the potentialities for leading students into new fields which belong to experiences already had, and must use that knowledge as his criterion for selection and arrangement of the conditions that influence their present experience" (Dewey, Experience and Education).

The teacher is the agent who is chiefly responsible for his highly complex process of education. It is his task to provide a setting conducive to learning, i.e. to prompt the development of ideas in the pupils. The teacher should be a catalytic agent, who, by providing materials, clues, information, suggestions, clarifications could create a setting that would be conducive to learning. In doing this he himself must become a learner. Dewey looks upon the relation between the teacher and the pupil as reciprocal. They should plan together and learn from each other. The teacher is not an authority in dispensing ideas to be absorbed by his pupils, but a guide, and a catalyst in getting the child to make his own relations and connections, his own ideas. In doing this, the modern teacher must take into consideration a great variety of factors that the traditional teachers considered extraneous. The total physical setting, since this, rather than merely the subject alone, makes up the environment for learning, the psychology of the individual pupils, so that differences in motivation, intelligence and orientation can be taken into account, the social psychology of the group, since general interests, needs and purposes will serve as the basis for developing the curriculum, the psychological principles of learning, memory, transfer and motivation, so that learning can be efficient and economical.

In order to accomplish all of this the teacher must be a well-educated professional. He must have a broad range of general knowledge on which to draw in developing units of instruction for his pupils. He must have a sound grounding in educational theory so that he understands the philosophical, psychological and sociological foundations of education. He must be able to see the reciprocal relation between theory and practice so that teaching is not reduced to a mere practical activity without grounding the theoretical science that has little relation to practice. "Teaching is a professional activity to the extent that it rests on principles of procedure. As the science of psychology matures this body of theory will become broader and deeper and the expertise of the teacher in promoting effective learning will become greater. Yet he will never become an authority in matters of morals or merely a model of conduct. His role is to be the chief agent for the liberation of the student". —John Dewey's Concept of Education.

Dewey began by defining the kind of school experiences that would help children to grow intellectually, ethically, emotionally, aesthetically, and spiritually. Teachers, who are sensitive to the conditions that could either foster or thwart such growth in their students, were needed. To assist them, they needed the valuable knowledge that could be gained only by personal professional experiences. They had to acquire the attitudes and skills that would enable them to continue learning about teaching even after they had become professionals. They need, in short, to become permanent students of education.

The teacher's effectiveness depends on his ability to interpret the meaning of his subject and to develop insights into the processes of inquiry that led to its creation. The teacher, who truly understands the significance of his subjects, may help students, through acts of appreciation, to share the sense of discovery of the creators of knowledge.

Some years later, Dewey elaborated the point when he considered the question of what is required for a teacher to become the intellectual leader of a group.

"The first condition goes back to his own intellectual preparation is subject matter. This should be abundant to the point of over flow. It must be much wider than the ground laid out in the text books or in any fixed plan for teaching a lesson. It must cover point so that the teacher can take advantage of unexpected questions or unanticipated incidents. It must be accompanied by a genuine enthusiasm for the subject that will communicate itself contagiously to pupils.

Some of the reasons why the teacher should have an excess supply of information and understanding are too obvious to need mention. The central reason is possibly not always recognised. The teacher must have his mind free to observe the mental responses and movements of the students members of the recitation group. The problem of the pupils is found in subject matter, the problems of teachers is what the minds of the pupils are doing with this subject matter in advance, unless it is thoroughly at home in it, using it unconsciously without the need of express thought, he will not be free to give full time and attention to observation and interpretation of the pupils intellectual reactions. The teacher must be alive to all forms of bodily expressions of mental condition, to puzzlement, boredom, mastery, the dawn of an idea, feigned attention tendency to show off, to dominate discussion because of egotism etc. as well as sensitive to the meaning of all expression in words. He must be aware not only of their meaning, but of their meaning as indicative of the state of mind of the pupil, his degree of observation and comprehension". (Dewey, How We Think? p. 274).

Dewey insistence that the teacher be a serious student of his subject is clear enough, but the quotation illustrates, too, his forceful insistence that the teachers obligation to advance the learning experiences of his students was the real task. The more the teacher is aware of the interests of his students and of the factors in their experience, the more imaginative he can be in establishing situations, raising questions, and suggesting activities that might engage students in an effort to make sense of things for themselves. This increases chances of effectively "reconstructing experience".

8

The Curriculum

Dewey's curriculum is not a mere scheme of studies, nor is it a list of subjects. It is an entire range of activities and experiences. For Dewey, subjects are only summaries and recapitulations of human activities. Dewey does not recommend any ready made curriculum. He rather wants the curriculum to grow out of the pupils' own impulses, interests and experiences. The curriculum consists of activities and projects, leading to reconstruction and reorganisation of experience. Thus, Dewey makes occupational activities or crafts, the core of school curriculum. He also includes moral, aesthetic and religious education in the curriculum. But this education is also imparted through practical experiences and not through 'chalk and talk lessons' in the classroom. In his opinion 'purposeful activity and a curriculum comprising standard factors of social life, would give the children more interest and insight, through the functioning of intelligence and will, in the achievement of self control and the appreciation of social values".

Dewey does not agree with the traditional curriculum. He does not like the division of knowledge into particular branches. He says "We violate the child's nature and render difficult the best ethical results by introducing the child too abruptly to a number of special studies of reading, writing, geography etc. According to Dewey, it is the child's own activities around which the school subjects should be organised and not around science, literature, history or geography. It is with the activities that the child has seen at home that the school should begin its work and not with teaching of reading, writing and arithmetic. Dewey says 'The beginning is made with child's expressive activities in dealing with the fundamental social material—housing (carpentry); clothing (sewing) food (cooking). These direct modes of expression...bring out...the factors of social communication—speech, writing, reading, drawing, moulding, etc. Thus the curriculum in the primary school should be organised according to the fourfold interests of the child-in conversation, inquiry, construction and artistic expression.

According to Dewey the curriculum should consist of educative experiences and problems. The aim is to enrich the already gained experiences and problems. The problems to be included in the curriculum should be so organised as to inspire the pupil to add to the existing knowledge and ideas. Dewey uses the words 'educative experiences' in a special sense. According to Dewey, only those experiences are educative which pay due regard to the natural inclinations of the child in the context of the social, political, physical and economic conditions of the community. Thus in Dewey's curriculum, books, teachers and apparatuses will be subordinated to the felt interests of the child.

Dewey suggests that the curriculum must develop critical discrimination in the pupil so that the latter may develop the capacity to choose intelligently from the various alternatives facing him. This is possible if the materials to be taught are taken from day to day life. The context of each subject should link the present with the past, at the same time the immediate usefulness of the context must be emphasised. Moreover, different subjects should not be presented at the particular branches of study. They should be correlated and linked together in such a way as to give the impression that they are items of a single process by which the continuance and growth of the society is assured.

"The social life of the child is the basis of concentration or correlation in all his training or growth. The social life gives the unconscious unity and the background of all his attainments. The subjects matter of the school curriculum should mark a gradual differentiation out of the primitive unconscious unity of social life". (Dewey, My Pedagogic Creed).

Dewey does not believe in the traditional philosophy of education, when it was believed that 'Sparing the rod would be spoiling the childs'. Traditional education, institutionalised in the grade school, with its system of credits, promotions and physical vindictive punishments, conceived of education as a one way procedure of handling down from above to below. It was preparation for life. For Dewey it is not so, education is not preparation for life but life itself. "Education must be carried on in forms worth living for their own sake". The good life is not a vision to be held before the pupil as a distant reward for enduring and suffering the hardships of education. The qualities of the good life should be inherent qualities of the educative process (Dewey, Education Today).

Dewey has always opposed the blossoming flower theory of education. For Dewey, the self is a product, a consequence of interracting in a social environment, of participating in social life and action. The school is a form of community life. The kind of self the child develops, the qualities of his mind and character will depend upon the kind of community the school is and upon the richness or poverty of the materials for growth it affords. So one may readily guess that Dewey had little sympathy for the traditional curriculum or any course of studies that divides knowledge into particular branches. According to Dewey social life cannot be cut into pieces of knowledge. Departmentalisation of the curriculum and the systematic succession of studies have been replaced by an electric programme of activities. He did not believe in a curriculum based on fixed knowledge, sub-divided logically into subjects to be completed in fixed intervals.

"There is nothing in the outer world corresponding to the departmentalisation of subject matter. It is only the logical interest of the adult that has divided the world into abstract compartments of knowledge. The objectives of learning are in future and its immediate materials are in present experience". "We may reject knowledge of the past as the end of education and thereby only emphasise its importance as a means" (Dewey, Experience and Education).

"Unless a given experience leads out into a field previously unfamiliar no problems arise, while problems are stimulus to thinking. The conditions found in the present experience should be used as sources of problems. The educator should see first, that the problems grows out of the conditions of the experience being had in the present, and what is within the range of the capacity of students. And secondly, that it is such that it arouses in the learners an active quest for information and for production of new ideas. The new facts and new ideas thus obtained become the ground for further experiences in which new problems are presented. (Dewey, Experience and Education).

Dewey points out that there are two essential factors in education—the individual and the social. "The task of educating so many children at so many different educational levels with the variety of abilities, needs and goals requires a completely different approach with this increase in diversified school population broader curricular programme are needed. Emphasis should be placed on the total development of the person as being equally important as the intellectual and the academic. Such a curriculum will acknowledge that the social responsibilities of education must present situations where problems are relevant to the problems of living together and where observation and information are calculated to develop social insight and interest."—Dewey.

"The individual factor in education necessitates taking the individual childs powers, interests and habits into consideration. The childs interests are diversified mainly in four directions, namely in conversation or communications inquiry or finding out things, construction or making things and artistic expression. Thus the primary root of all educative activity is in the instinctive, impulsive attitudes and activities of the child, and not in the presentation and application of external material. But these powers, habits and interests are never isolated, they get activised only against a social background". (Dewey, My Pedagogic Creed).

"It is a sound educational principle that students should be introduced to scientific subject matter and be initiated into its facts and laws through acquaintance with everyday social applications. Adherence to this method is not only the most direct avenue to the understanding of science itself but as the pupils grow more mature it is also the surest road to the understanding of the economic and industrial problems of the present society".

"The methods of science also point the way to the measures and politics by means of which a better social order can be brought into existence".

"Dewey condemned the undue importance given to book learning and said that learning, in order to be capable of leading the child the learning, should be related to the actual life of the child. The school life of the child was to be an indistinguishable part of its normal life. While the previous epoch emphasised the inclinations of the child as the basis of educational methodology. Dewey took his stand on the needs of the child as a real living member of the society. This pattern may be called life-centred education. To help the child there should be continuity between the schools activities and basic aspects of the out of school world. The school should also, in the pattern of its life develop, the values and qualities of human relations that promote growth, the ways of learning and living and should demonstrate habits of cooperation, free communication and reflective thinking—The theory held that values were learnt better when they were lived than when they were merely talked about. Dewey believed that if education is imparted according to right principles the child will become suitable for social life when he becomes an adult". (G. Wirth, John Dewey as an educator, p. 125).

The mind of the child is a complete unity and not divided into water tight compartments. With such a practical approach to curriculum. Dewey gives his scheme of education based upon the following stages:

1. Play period from 4 to 8 years of age.
2. Period of spontaneous attention from 8 to 12 years of age.
3. Period of reflective attention from 12 years onwards.

Although this clearly shows that he indicated no order of preferences for classifying human activities, he says "that the curriculum" must be planned with reference to placing essentials first and refinements second". His essentials are man's fundamental concerns like food, shelter, clothing, household furnishing and the appliances connected with production, exchange and consumption. He made industrial activities and their historical and social development the centre of the curriculum and grouped the rest of the studies around this centre.

"It is a cardinal precept of the newer school of education that the beginning of instruction shall be made with the experience learners already have, this experience and the capacities have been developed during its course provide the starting point for all further learning".

Orderly development towards expansion and organisation of subject matter through growth of experience".

The school should not begin with the 3Rs. But with the activities that the child has seen in the house, the activities that constitute the great racial functions. In the primary school, Dewey began with the activities with which the child is familiar in home life, getting food, shelter and clothing. These activities make the most natural appeals to his interest. They arouse the constructive instinct and bring out not only nerve and muscular coordination's but all aspects of mentality into functional action. In the first six grades Dewey emphasised numbers, music, art, woodwork, cooking experiences (and this means that there some advance be made in conscious articulation of facts and idea), sewing, science, geography, reading, writing, history and gardening. It must be understood, however, that all of these were learnt in connection with the production of food, shelter and clothing. By these constructive activities, the attention of the child was directed to the actual world, where he learnt from observation, agriculture, transportation, industrial activities and the problems of distribution, the buying and selling of commodities. He was led back into history to find the origin of all these activities in primitive life. In his constructive activity the child acquired the fact of arithmetic, geography, history, botany, chemistry the use of language and other formal subjects.

Aesthetic, moral and religious education was not omitted by Dewey from his curriculum. For full development he considered art as 'perfected expression of basic human activity. Similarly he wants the moral and religious education to be an integrated part of the basic experiences of the child. He hates those systems which claim to have character development as their main aim and yet in practice they do nothing to develop the character. He does not want to give religious and moral education through lessons but by practical experience purposeful activity and a curriculum comprising of standard factors of social life in his opinion, would give the children moral interest and insight, "through the functioning of intelligence and will in the achievement of self control and the appreciation of social values" (V.R. Taneja, 1983, p. 150-51).

According to Dewey "a religion can be realised itself only through science that is through ways of understanding human nature in its concrete actuality and of discovering how its various factors are modified by interaction with the variety of conditions under which they operate. Without science this religion is bound to become formal hypocritical and a mass of dogmas". (Dewey, Education Today, pp. 148-149).

9

The Discipline

"Discipline means power at command, mastery of resources available for carrying through the action undertaken. To know what one is to do and move to do it promptly and by use of the requisite means is to be disciplined, whether we are thinking of an army or a mind. Discipline is positive to cow the spirit, to subdue inclination, to compel obedience, to mortify the flesh, to make a subordinate perform an uncogenial task—these things are not disciplinary according, as they do or do not tend to the development of power to recognise what one is about and persistence in accomplishment" (Dewey, Democracy and Education).

Dewey believes in free discipline, which is not based on punishments and rewards or outer control. It is self discipline resulting from free, purposeful and creative activities. John Dewey says 'The natural way of establishing such a discipline is to redirect the natural impulses of children, through cooperative or shared activities, along socially approved lines, for the realisation of certain definite purposes. In such activities, each child realises his responsibility and acquires self discipline". Dewey says that the real purpose of school discipline is to cultivate such habits through activities of the school so as to improve both the individual and the social efficiency.

It was to give his ideals a practical shape that Dewey started a Laboratory or experimental School in Chicago in 1896. The main aim was "to carry research and experiment in new ideas and methods of education and to create conditions for the discovery of more natural ways to teaching and learning". About this school, Dewey himself said "in intent, whatever the failure in accomplishment, the school was community centred".

Being against the traditional concept of discipline Dewey advocated 'self discipline'. Such a discipline, that is free discipline, results out of free, purposeful and creative activities. There activities must be cooperative. Dewey's concept of self discipline reflects democratic society. The role of the teacher would not be disciplining the students but providing right kind of environment so that every child may find ample scope to develop himself in terms of a responsible member of the society, group or community. The teacher is not to impose himself upon the students. He is not to be discipline conscious—The chief aim of discipline is to develop social attitudes, social interests, social habits and social will. Through social discipline Dewey wants to direct the natural inclinations of the child through cooperative activities of the school. Through such a kind of training the child will develop a character which will be individually satisfying and socially useful. Dewey believes that if the child's activities are purposeful and are carried out in cooperation with others, they will be disciplinary in their effect. If there are common goals to be achieved, the relations among the various pupils in the school will be automatically characterised by discipline.

Dewey does realise the necessity of discipline in the school as a precondition for smooth work. But he holds that the discipline should not be aimed at as end in itself. Respect for authority, patience and endurance have their place in life, but they should be the result of the child's appreciation of the value of leadership and necessity of rule and law in the school. No attempt should be made to develop them for their own sake. The purpose of discipline in school according to Dewey is to produce a socialised individual who is conscious to develop himself fully and is always prepared to contribute his share to the social good. In his concept of discipline Dewey has been influenced very greatly by both Froebel and Herbart.

"The inclusion of students in the idea of freedom of education is even more important than the inclusion of teachers". Dewey prefers "democratic and human arrangements to those which are autocratic and harsh". One cause may be that we have been taught not only in the schools but by the press, the pulpit, the platform, and our laws and law-making bodies that democracy is best of all social institutions. (Dewey, Experience and Education, p. 25).

"Education is a necessary condition for creation of the kind of citizenship indispensable to the success of democracy". (Ibid. p. 322).

"Since freedom of mind and freedom of expression are the root of all freedom, to deny freedom in education is a crime against democracy. Academic freedom is so essentially a social issues since it is intimately bound up with what the future citizenship of the country is going to do in shaping our political and economic destiny". (Ibid. p. 322).

"The foundation of democracy is faith in the capacities of human natures, faith in human intelligence. It is not belief that those things are complete but, that, if given a show they will grow and be able to generate progressively the knowledge and wisdom needed to guide collective action". (Ibid. p. 330).

Dewey emphasised democratic and human ideas because he is in view that "the prevalence of methods of authority and of external dictation and direction tends automatically to perpetuate the very conditions of inefficiency, lack of interests, inability to assume positions of self-determination, which constitute the reasons that are depended upon to justify the regime of authority". (Ibid p. 67).

"There is no discipline in the world so serve as the discipline of experience subjected to the tests of intelligent development and direction". (Dewey, Experience and Education, p. 114).

If, in a school, children are given opportunities of working according to their aptitudes and interests, there will be no problem of discipline. "The aim of the methods must be to develop individualists, to let the children do as they please. These methods were in fact, introduced because we know that physical freedom is necessary to growing bodies and because psychological investigations have proved that learning is better and faster when the learner understands his problem as a whole and does his work under his own motive power than under minute piece meal dictation from a boss". (Ibid, p. 278).

In Dewey's words the standards for discipline is—"Its aim is the kind of order that exists in a roomful of people, each one of whom is working at a common task. There will be talking, consulting, moving about in such a group, whether the workers are adults or children. The standard for order and discipline of a group is not how silent is the room, or how few and uniform the kinds of tools and material that are being used, but the quality and amount of work done by the individuals and the group". (Ibid. p. 277).

"What the argument for democracy implies is that the best way to produce initiative and constructive power is to exercise its power as well as interest, come by use and practice". (Ibid, p. 345).

Dewey emphasised on the social controls as well as individual freedom, that is social control of individual without the violation of freedom. In a well ordered school the main reliance for control of this and that individual is upon the activities carried on and upon the situations in which these activities are maintained. Children learn the difference when playing with one another. (Ibid. pp. 58-60).

The primary source of social control resides in the very nature of the work done as a social enterprise in which all individuals have an opportunity to contribute and to which all feel a responsibility. Most children are naturally sociable. Isolation is even more irksome to them than to adults. A genuine community life has its ground in this natural sociability. But community life does not organise itself in an enduring way purely spontaneously. It requires plan ahead. The educator is responsible for a knowledge of individuals and for a knowledge of subject matter, that will enable activities to be selected which lend themselves to social organisation, an organisation in which all individuals have an opportunity to contribute something, and in which the activities are the chief carriers of control'. (Ibid, p. 62).

The teacher should not consider himself superior to the child, should not give any sermons, instead should only supervise the work of the child. The teacher should stimulate the natural aptitude of the child and should channelise them in a useful work. The individual interests of children are not similar, they are different. The teacher should understand the individual differences in children.

"The teacher must survey the capacities and needs of the particular set of individuals with whom he is dealing and must at the same time arrange the conditions which provide the subject matter or content for experiences that satisfy these needs and develop these capacities. The planning must be flexible enough to permit free play for individuality of experience and yet firm enough to give direction towards continuous development of power." (Ibid, p. 65).

"The teacher's business is to see that the occasion is taken advantage of since freedom resides in the operations of intelligent observation and judgement by which a purpose is developed. Guidance given by the teacher to the exercise of the pupils intelligence is an aid to freedom not a restriction upon it". (Ibid, p. 84).

"The ideal aim of education is creation of power of self control". It is the teacher's responsibility to ensure that the individual and the group move in harmony. "Both acquiring the best and most positive habits of growth". Instead of establishing rigid discipline, the teacher must observe, plan and encourage self discipline develop through the will of the pupils, themselves.

There are likely to be some, who, when they come to school, are already victims of injurious conditions outside the school and who have become so passive and unduly decide that they fail to contribute. Dewey did not give too much importance to these exceptional cases. It is much more likely to arise from failure to arrange advance for the kind of work which will create situations that by themselves tend to exercise control over what this, that and other pupil does and how he does it. The failure often goes back to lack of sufficiently throughout planning in advance".

"Failure to take into account adaptation to the needs and capacities of individuals was the source of the idea that certain subjects and certain methods are intrinsically cultural or good for mental discipline". (Dewey, Experience and Education, p. 46).

"So the teacher should arrange conditions that are conducive to the community activity and to organisation which exercises control over individual impulses".

Dewey gave three principles upon which progressive schools work.

1. They all aim at greater attention to distinctively individual needs and characteristics. Hence, they are provided by a great degree of freedom of action and discussion.
2. They aim at an unwanted amount of co-operation of pupils with one another, and of pupils with teachers. The latter function and follows—workers in the activities that are going on rather than as rulers set on high. This fact determines that distinctive character of discipline in progressive schools.

It is meant to be self-discipline as far it is possible, gained through sharing in work and play in which all have a common interest. "The discipline of the schools as a whole and not directly from the teacher". (Dewey, My Pedagogic Creed).

Education is a social process and school is a social institution. This will enable them to meet their social obligations. It is also concerned to bring the child to share the interested resources of the race and to use his own power for social ends. School is a miniature society. It is a place where children learn to live as members of school community, which represent the community as a whole. It is therefore necessary that the school should essentially take up and continue the activities with which the child is already familiar in the home.

10

The Values

According to John Dewey "Values are as unstable as the forms of clouds. They keep on changing from time to time and reality is still in the process of making. Ideal ends are remotely connected with immediate and urgent conditions. Men naturally devote themselves to the present conditions than the remote".

The main principle of John Dewey's philosophy, that is, pragmatism, is that men creates his own values during the course of an activity. There are no fixed values for all times to come. Even truths are man-made products. There is nothing like an absolute truth. Whatever fulfils man's purposes and desires and develops his life, is true. Truth is that, which gives satisfactory results when put into practice.

"For example the way to enable to student to apprehend the instrumental value of arithmetic, is not to lecture him upon the benefit it will be to him in some remote and uncertain future, but to let him discover that success in something he is interested in doing upon ability to use number". (Dewey, Democracy and Education, p. 240).

Similarly, Science may have any kind of value, depending upon the situation into which it enters as a means it may be military, commercial, philanthropic value are those which are utilitarian (Ibid, p. 244).

Usefulness of anything is the most important thing according to John Dewey. The value of experimentation is very important. Every statement needs to be tested and the practical implications have to be found out. Basing on the desirability of the implications the statement is accepted or rejected. Only that things is good and beautiful which emerged out useful after experimentation.

Dewey, as a pragmatist, does not believe in the wisdom of the past or age old values. John Dewey says "Philosophy, in order to be philosophy, should have meaning and utility in the solution of human problems. It should be practical and useful in influencing the conduct of life and not passive enquiry or contemplation". (Safaya and Shaida, 1963).

Value of adjustment is one of the most important according to John Dewey. Not only does man adjust himself to the environment, but he also moulds the environment according to his needs, purposes and desires.

Values of democracy are of great great importance to John Dewey, the world known pragmatist, almost a fore-runner of pragmatism. According to Dewey, it is only through democracy that an individual can realise the maximum development of his personality. The general aim of education according to him is the creation of new values. The educator should educate the individual to develop values for himself. For the creation of new values, activity and experience are important. Education should provide physical, intellectual, moral and aesthetic activities as the media for the creation of values.

Values according to Dewey are obtained in the society—they emerge only in individual and social flow of events. Values are forever in a state of flux. Unlike any of the idealists, Dewey, a pragmatist, does not believe in eternal and ultimate values. He says they are relative to situations and times. At the same time

Dewey's philosophy, pragmatism, is based on the concept of human values. It locates and identifies values in the human experiences. It is therefore called Humanism. Dewey's emphasis, is on the present. He does not believe in absolute truths, according to him truth is that which works. "To seek truth or values of life beyond human experiences into the supernatural world of man's fancy is futile." Life is full of concrete situations facing concrete problems which require constructive solutions based on the philosophy of practice and practical judgement.

John Dewey shows firm and deep faith in democracy, as democracy is a way of life and a spirit of sharing experiences. It is this sharing of experiences that enables individuals to develop an understanding of other people and their attitudes. Life, education and democratic process are all rolled into one and these will definitely develop all the democratic values in people.

Since pragmatism in spirit is naturalistic, in method scientific and practical, and purpose social and human, it strongly believes in the reality of change over permanence, the relatively of values, the social and biological nature of man, the importance of democracy as a way of life, the value of critical intelligence in all human conduction etc.

John Dewey is against higher and spiritual values. According to him every thing is provisional, nothing is ultimate, knowledge is a means and never an end in itself". He stressed on the importance of physical and social environment and he believed that an individual can grow fully only by interacting with the others in the society and adjusting them and himself. The value of adjustment, cooperation team spirit work mindedness usefulness, are all important. Dewey experienced that the barriers of caste, colour, religion language etc. divided humanity. These barriers must be broken to establish harmony between individuals and groups". The aim of living is ever enduring process of perfecting and refining". He advocated co-operative and associated living social virtues are of greatest importance to Dewey—Even the methods of education propagated by Dewey help in the development of such virtues.

11

Summary

Biographical Sketch of John Dewey

John Dewey, the American philosopher, psychologist, practical teacher and one of the greatest thinkers of his age, was born in 1859. He was brought up in a rural environment. He had his school education in the ordinary public school of the locality where he lived. He got his Ph.D in 1881 and worked as a teacher for a few years. In 1884 he became an instructor in the University of Michigan. In 1894 he was appointed as the head of the department of philosophy at the University of Chicago. From 1902 to 1904, he was also the Director of the School Education. In 1896, he founded his 'laboratory school' in the University of Chicago, which brought him world fame. In 1904, he was appointed as the professor of philosophy in the University of Columbia and he held this post till 1930. After that too, he remained there as a professor until he died in 1952. During these years, he was invited by many countries to suggest the ways to reorganise schools. So he influenced the course of education by his ideas. John Dewey has been universally accepted as a great humanist and a great educator. He had exercised a profound influence on the schools of not only America but also other countries. He had lectures in Japan, Turkey, China, Russia, etc., on several problems of education. Dewey enjoyed universal honour and fame. His educational ideas were expressed in his books and articles which he wrote in large numbers and volumes.

Being brought up in a rural environment, John Dewey realised from the very beginning that traditional methods of instruction were not at all effective and that social contracts of everyday life provided effective dynamic and unlimited learning situations. These very ideas formed the foundation of the educational theory formulated later by him. His outlook on education reflected the Industrial Revolution and the Development of Democracy. He believed in the dynamic nature of things and values. Dewey changed with change in ideas as a result of experience and experimentation and finally emerged as pragmatist.

Dewey's Philosophy of Life

For those who believe it is the philosopher's task to juggle the universe on the point of an argument, Dewey is a complete disappointment. The world, he starts out with and also ends with, is the common world we all live in and experience everyday of our lives. Dewey's philosophy and programme have been variously termed as Experimentalism, Functionalism, Instrumentalism, Operationalism, Progressivism, Practicalism, and above all Pragmatism. All these indicate his emphasis on the dynamic and ever changing character of life.

Dewey does not see any difference between knowledge and experience. According to him, knowledge is only a result of our various types of experiences. He does not believe in any pre-determined truths. He does not accept the permanence of truth of reality for ever. His chief importance lies in his criticism of the traditional notion of truths, which is embodied in the theory he calls 'Intuitonalism'.

Dewey's philosophy is fundamentally derivative from his analysis of the scientific method. According to him, philosophy, to be significant and intelligent, must be scientific, that is, must follow in its inquiries the method of science. Dewey takes modern science as exemplar of what knowledge is and the method of modern science as a standard method of knowing. Dewey turned exclusively towards the natural sciences. The key notions of Dewey's idea of the scientific method of thinking and control, experiment and objective test.

His aim is to bring the scientific method of reflective thought to all phases of human activity, including politics, art and morals. It was not only the actual content and method of science that interested Dewey but the connotations that were associated with science, that is, objectivity, honesty, freedom, open-mindedness, etc. According to him, philosophy was to follow the spirit of science not only in it's approach to problems of metaphysics and epistemology but also in the fields of ethics and aesthetic. Dewey saw democracy as the political manifestation of the scientific method.

He did not consider any object or idea permanent. He believed in social change. He did not believe in any divine power, but had a strong faith in the power of man. He said that man will have to make his own path for his development and progress, hence, he has to depend on his creative intelligence. Dewey always thought of philosophy in culture, not of philosophy and culture. Dewey introduced a new spirit into modern philosophy which is invaluable.

Dewey's Concept of Education

According to Dewey, every child is born with certain capacities and powers and education is the development of all those capacities in the individual which will enable him to control his environment and fulfill his responsibilities. Education is a social necessity. It is the necessity of life. All education proceeds by the participation of the individual in the social consciousness of the race. He believed that collective work enables the child to understand the aim and purpose of work and gives him necessary methods and ability to do that work. Education, for Dewey, is not preparation for life, but life itself. Education is growth.

According to Dewey, education is a bi-polar process, one is psychological and the other sociological. He recognised the individual differences and took into consideration the impulses and interests of the child when he expounded his theories of education. These capacities and instincts should be brought in to exercise in the social situations. He said that the purpose of education was to give the young, the things they need, in order to develop in an orderly sequential way, to be members of a society. He emphasised learning by doing. He gave much importance to activity. According to him, the educative process would be haphazard without insight into the psychological structure and activity of the individual. The purpose of education is to create harmony between the individual and social development.

Dewey emphasised experience, experiment, purposeful learning, freedom, and other well-known concepts of "progressive education". He interprets education as the scientific method by means of which man studies the world, acquires cumulatively, knowledge of means and values.

According to him, education is a process of reconstruction of experience, giving it a more socialised value through the medium of increased social efficiency. This experience comes through interaction with one another. He says that every experience should do something to prepare a person for later experiences of a deeper and more expensive nature. A full-integrated personality on the other hand exists only when experiences are integrated with one another.

Dewey's Aims of Education

According to Dewey, there are no ultimate and fixed aims of education, they are rather proximate. Education proceeds by constantly remarking experience and it is the reconstruction which constitutes its value and accomplishes its aim. The continuous enrichment of experience by adjusting to the complexities of the environment, constitutes the heart of education. According to him, the aim of education is the development of reflective, creative and responsible thought.

Education must be imparted according to the individual needs of the child. 'Social efficiency' is the aim of education according to Dewey. In Dewey's theory, society is an organic union of individuals Education should proceed by the participation of the individual in social relationships with his fellow human beings. The school should include individual and social goals. The aim of education should be to serve to secure a balance interaction of the practical and theoretical attitudes. The other aim of education is that it should train the individual for specific adult life. Dewey agreed that 'Self-realisation' is an important aim of education. He even accepted 'cultural aim' as an important aim of education. Expression even accepted 'cultural aim' as an important aim of education. Expression and cultivation of individuality, free activity, learning through experience, acquisition of skills and techniques, making use of most of the opportunities of present life, and acquaintance with a changing world are the aim of education according to John Dewey.

Dewey's Methods of Teaching and Learning

Dewey believed that true education comes through the stimulation of the child's powers by the demands of the social situations in which the child finds himself. Dewey drew the attention of the public, to the urgent need to stop rote learning and integrate the school with society and the curriculum with home. He condemned the undue importance given to book learning and said that learning should come through activities. The activities should be related to the actual life of the child and for this he advocated the introduction of adult occupations. He insisted on 'learning by doing'. He emphasised on the well-known method of reasoning according to inductive logic. The project method is the practical outcome of Dewey's philosophy.

The project method translates the idea of education through occupations into a form suitable for the ordinary school. The project method is that method of teaching which encourages a maximum amount of purposeful activity on the part of the pupils.

The problem comes first and learning in incidental to its successful solution. Principles, skills and methods are acquired by the pupil as the experiences the need for them.

According to Dewey, interests are the signs and symptoms of growing power. Accordingly, the constant and careful observation of interests is of utmost importance to the education.

Dewey insisted upon direct experience, not only did he demand that concrete situations be furnished for the child in order to call forth the child's activity but he insisted that all learning should come to the child as a by-product of his actions and never as something to be learnt directly for it's own sake. He believed that learning proceeds from concrete to the general. Uniform methods cannot possibly produce uniform results in education, hence the methods should be individualised.

Dewey's Concept of the Role of Teacher

A Deweyan teacher should be concerned with his pupils' impulses and interests rather than the inculcation of knowledge. His function is to guide the young through the complexities of life. For this, the teacher should provide them opportunities to learn in the natural way.

John Dewey believed in giving the child great freedom, but the teacher has to regulate it. Since he is ahead of his pupils in experience, he should survey the social heritage and look to a more distant purpose than his pupil. The teacher must ensure that the individual and the group move in harmony both acquiring the best and most positive habits of growth. The teacher must guide the young not only the habit of democratic co-operation, but also towards the highest intellectual pursuits and the fullest aesthetic experience. Dewey did not want any autocracy in the school. The teacher must know the individual differences in the children.

The teacher should not consider himself superior to child. For Dewey, the development of the child should be according to the social environment. The teachers must be familiar with the social situation because that would enable him to interpret properly, the child's activities and transfer them into social channels. The teacher should not impose faiths or try to form rigid habits in the child, but he should select the proper influences for the child and assist him in responding to them.

The teachers should try to understand the child sympathetically. The teacher should become a permanent student of education he should have an excess to supply of information and understanding.

Dewey's Concept of Curriculum

According to Dewey, the organisation of the study and the methods of teaching for each phase of the child, must be such that the process of learning will satisfy the needs, enrich the qualities and nurture the powers of the individual. So, Dewey did not believe in a curriculum based on fixed knowledge. According to him, it must be flexible. It should grow out of pupils? Interests, impulses and experiences. It should, therefore, consists of activities and projects leading to reconstruction of experience. The primary root of all educative activity is in the instinctive and impulsive attitudes and activities of the child and not in the presentation and application of external material.

Since the main hypothesis of Dewey was itself, he advocated the introduction of adult occupations and associations, which serve the needs of man, as the core around which the entire curriculum should be built. To help the child, there should be a continuity between the school activities and the basic aspects of the out-of-school world. The school should also represent, in the pattern of its life, the values and qualities of human relations that promote growth. Thus, according to Dewey, the school curriculum must be organised around the child's activities and not subject.

The curriculum must be planned with reference to placing essentials first and refinements second. The second not begin with the 3Rs but with the activities that the child has seen at home, the activities that constitute the great racial functions.

Aesthetic, moral and religious education was not omitted by Dewey from his curriculum. He does not want to give religious and moral education through lessons but by practical experience. Purposeful activity and a curriculum comprising standard factors of social life, in his opinion, would give the children moral interest and insight. According to Dewey, a religion can be realised itself only through science, without science, religion is bound to become formal, hypocritical and a mass of dogmas.

Dewey's Concept of Discipline

According to Dewey, children are individuals whose freedom should be respected. The new education emphasises the freedom of the learner and aims at greater attention to distinctive individual needs and characteristics. Hence, they are provided by a great degree of freedom of action and discussion.

According to him if, in a school, children are given opportunities of working according to their aptitudes and interests, there will be no problem of discipline. For Dewey, the standard for discipline is not how silent a classroom is or how few and uniform the kinds of tools and materials that are being used, but the amount of quality work done by the individuals and the group. He emphasised individual freedom and social control. Control of the individuals without the violation of freedom, according to him, is the primary source of social control. It requires planning ahead. Instead of establishing rigid discipline, the teacher must observe, plan, and encourage. Weakness in control, found in progressive schools, arises because of the lack of sufficiently thought out planning in advance. So, the teacher should arrange conditions that are conducive to community activity and to organisation which exercises control over individual impulses by the mere fact that all are engaged in communal projects. According to Dewey, the ideal aim of education is creation of power of self control. Self discipline and group discipline develop through the will of the pupils themselves. Progressive schools aim at unwanted amount of co-operation of pupils with one another, and of pupils with teachers.

According to Dewey, through the functioning of will in the achievement of self control and the application of social values, children will themselves develop morally in a social environment through natural activities.

Dewey's Concept of Values

According to Dewey, "values are as unstable as the forms of clouds. They keep on changing from time to time and reality is still in the process of making. Ideal ends are remotely connected with immediate and urgent conditions. Man naturally devote themselves to the present conditions than the remote".

There are no fixed values for all times. Even truths are man-made products. There is nothing like an absolute truth. Whatever fulfils, man's purposes and desires and develops his life, is true. Truth is that which gives satisfactory results when put into practice.

Values of democracy are of great importance to John Dewey. According to him, it is only through democracy that an individual can realise the maximum development of his personality. The general aim of education, according to Dewey, is the creation of new values. The educator should educate the individuals to develop values for himself. For the creation of new values, activity and experience are important. Education should provide physical, intellectual, moral and aesthetic activities as the media for the creation of values.

Values, according to Dewey, are obtained in the society as they emerge only in individual and social flow of events. Values are forever in a state of flux. They are relative to place and time. Pragmatism is based on the concept of human values. As pragmatism locates and identifies values in human experiences, it is also called humanism. "To seek truth or values of life beyond human experiences into super natural world of man's facy is futile", says Dewey.

Dewey's pragmatism, in spirit it is naturalistic, in method it is scientific and practical, in purpose it is social and human. It strongly believes in the reality of change over permanence, the relativity of values, the social and biological nature of man, the importance of democracy as a way of life, the value of critical intelligence in all human conduction etc., Social virtues are of great importance to John Dewey.

Bibliography

Aggarwal, J.C. (1967), *Thoughts on Education*, Arya Book Depot, New Delhi.

Bhatia, K.K. and Narang, C.L. (1979), *Principles of Education*, Prakash Brothers, Ludhiana.

Bhatia, K.K. and Narang, C.L. (1985). *Philosophical and Sociological Foundations of Education*, Prakash Brothers Educational Publishers, Ludhiana.

Bhatt, K.K. (1986). *Knowledge, Values and Education*, Gian Publishing House.

Biswas, A. and Aggarwal, J.C. (1968). *Some Indian Educationalists*, Asha Prakashan Griha, New Delhi.

Blair, L., Joseph. *Men and Movements in American Philosophy*, Prentice Hall Inc, Englewood Cliffs, N.J.

Brubacher, S. John. (1969). *Modern Philosophers of Education*, Tata, Mc Graw Hill Publishing Company, Bombay.

Chaube, S.P. (1988). *Indian and Western Educational Philosophers*, Vinod Pusthak Mandir, Agra.

Chaube, S.P. (1990). *Philosophical and Sociological Foundations of Education*, Vinod Pusthak Mandir, Agra.

Chester, W. (1960), *Encyclopaedia of Education Research*, The Mac Millan Company, New York.

Clement, C.J. and Cumberlege, Web Geoffrey. *A History of Philosophy*, Oxford University Press, London.

Damodaran, K. *Indian Thought—A Critical Survey*, Asia Publishing House—Bombay.

Dewey, John, (1910), *How We Think*, D.C. Health and Co. New York.

Dewey John, (1915), *The School and Society—Revised Edition*, University of Chicago Press, Chicago.

Dewey, John (1915), *Schools of Tomorrow*, E.P. Dutton, New York.

Dewey, John (1916), *Democracy and Education*, The Mac Millan Co-New York.

Dewey, John (1922), *Human Nature and Conduct*, An Introduction to Social Psychology, Henry Holt and Company—New York.

Dewey, John (1939). *Intelligence in the Modern World (John Dewey's Philosophy)*. The Modern Library, New York.

Dewey, John (1940). *Education Today*, G.P. Putman's Sons, New York.

Dewey, John (1946), *Experience and Education*, The Mac Millan Co. New York.

Dewey, John (1964). *Freedom and Culture*, Bhavan's Book University Series.

Dewey, John, *Experience and Nature*, Oxford Book Company, Calcutta.

Dewey, John, *My Pedagogic Creed–Article III*, The Progressive Education Association, Washington, D.C.

Lee, C. Deighton (Ed) (1971): *The Encyclopaedia of Education*, Volume 10, The Mac Millan Co. & Free Press, U.S.A.

Magill, N. Frank (Ed) *Master Pieces of World Philosophy in Summary Form,* George Allen and Unwin Ltd., Ruskin House. Museum Street, London.

Peter Freund, B. Sheldon and Thedore, C. Denise. *Contemporary Philosophy and it's Origins. Text and Readings (An East and West Edition),* D. Van Nostrand Company Inc, Princeton—New Jersey.

Ramanadhan, G. (1962), *Education from Dewey to Gandhi,* Asia Publishing House, New Delhi.

Thomas, George and White, Patrick, *Introduction to Philosophy,* Revised Edition, Ruskin House, George Allen and Unwin Ltd., Museum Street, London.

Titus, H. Harold, *Living Issues in Philosophy,* III Edition, American Book Company, New York.

Torcata, C. Lourenco (1970), *Education, Its History and Philosophy,* Jack Printers, Bombay.

Verma, K.K. (1969), *Educational and Philosophical Thoughts.* The Indian Publication, Ambala Cantt. India.

Whitehead, N. Alfred (1929). *The Aims of Education and Other Essays,* Mac Millan, New York.

Wirth, G. Arthur (1969), *John Dewey As An Educator,* Wiley Eastern Pvt. Ltd., New Delhi.

Additional Reading

Bhaskara Rao, Digumarti (1994). *Scientific Aptitude*. New Delhi: Ashish Publishing House. ISBN 81-7024-658-X.

Bhaskara Rao, Digumarti (1995). *Animal Kingdom*. New Delhi: Discovery Publishing House. ISBN 81-7141-274-2.

Bhaskara Rao, Digumarti (1995). *Batracology*. New Delhi: Discovery Publishing House. ISBN 81-7141-279-3.

Bhaskara Rao, Digumarti (1997). *Scientific Attitude*. New Delhi: Discovery Publishing House. ISBN 81-7141-381-1.

Bhaskara Rao, Digumarti (1996). *Scientific Attitude vis-à-vis Scientific Aptitude*. New Delhi: Discovery Publishing House. ISBN 81-7141-308-0.

Bhaskara Rao, Digumarti (2004). *Scientific Attitude, Scientific Aptitude and Achievement*. New Delhi: Discovery Publishing House. ISBN 81-7141-781-7.

Bhaskara Rao, Digumarti (2004). *Educational Administration*. New Delhi: Discovery Publishing House. ISBN 81-7141-842-2.

Bhaskara Rao, Digumarti, editor (1996). *Encyclopaedia of Education For All*, 5 volumes. New Delhi: APH Publishing Corporation. ISBN 81-7024-759-4 (set).

Vol. I *Education For All: The World Conference*. ISBN 81-7024-760-8

Vol. II *Education For All: The EPA-9 Summit*. ISBN 81-7024-761-6

Vol. II *Education For All: Quality Education For All*. ISBN 81-7024-762-6.

Vol. IV *Education For All: Planning and Monitoring*. ISBN 81-7024-763-4.

Vol. V *Education For All: The Indian Scenario*. ISBN 81-7024-764-0.

Bhaskara Rao, Digumarti, editor (1996). *Global Perceptions on Peace Education*, 3 volumes. New Delhi: Discovery Publishing House. ISBN 81-7141-319-6.

Bhaskara Rao, Digumarti, editor (1996). *National Policy on Education*, 2 volumes. New Delhi: Anmol Publications Pvt. Ltd. ISBN 81-7488-323-1.

Bhaskara Rao, Digumarti, editor (1997). *Care the Child*, 2 volumes. New Delhi: Discovery Publishing House. ISBN 81-7141-394-3.

Bhaskara Rao, Digumarti, editor (1997). *Education for the 21st Century*. New Delhi: Discovery Publishing House. ISBN 81-7141-389-7.

Bhaskara Rao, Digumarti, editor (1997). *Reflections on Scientific Attitude*. New Delhi: Discovery Publishing House. ISBN 81-7141-319-6.

Bhaskara Rao, Digumarti, editor (1997). *Success Story of a Primary Education Project*. New Delhi: APH Publishing Corporation. ISBN 81-7024-850-7.

Bhaskara Rao, Digumarti, editor (1997). *World Food Summit*. New Delhi: Discovery Publishing House. ISBN 81-7141-386-2.

Bhaskara Rao, Digumarti, editor (1998). *Adolescence Education*. New Delhi: Discovery Publishing House. ISBN 81-7141-432-X.

Bhaskara Rao, Digumarti, editor (1998). *Community and School Nutrition Education*. New Delhi: Discovery Publishing House. ISBN 81-7141-435-4.

Bhaskara Rao, Digumarti, editor (1998). *District Primary Education Programme*. New Delhi: Discovery Publishing House. ISBN 81-7141-396-X.

Bhaskara Rao, Digumarti, editor (1998). *Earth Summit*, 2 volumes. New Delhi: Discovery Publishing House. ISBN 81-7141-435-4.

Bhaskara Rao, Digumarti, editor (1998). *National Policy on Education: Towards an Enlightened and Humane Society*. New Delhi: Discovery Publishing House. ISBN 81-7141-426-5.

Bhaskara Rao, Digumarti, editor (1998). *Reforming School Education*. New Delhi: Discovery Publishing House. ISBN 81-7141-403-6.

Bhaskara Rao, Digumarti, editor (1998). *Teacher Education in India*. New Delhi: Discovery Publishing House. ISBN 81-7141-406-0.

Bhaskara Rao, Digumarti, editor (1998). *World Summit for Social Development*. New Delhi: Discovery Publishing House. ISBN 81-7141-420-6.

Bhaskara Rao, Digumarti, editor (2000). *Education For All: Achieving the Goal*, 3 volumes. New Delhi: APH Publishing Corporation. ISBN 81-7648-152-1 (set).

Vol. I *The Global Consensus*. ISBN 81-7648-155-6.

Vol. II *Mid-Decade Review Reports of Regional Seminars*. ISBN 81-7648-154-8.

Vol. III *Issues and Trends*. ISBN 81-7648-155-6.

Bhaskara Rao, Digumarti, editor (1999). *International Encyclopaedia of AIDS*, 11 volumes. New Delhi: Discovery Publishing House. ISBN 81-7141-522-6 (set).

Vol. 1 *Introduction to HIV/AIDS*. ISBN 81-7141-523-7.

Vol. 2 *HIV/AIDS—Issues and Challenges*, 2 parts. ISBN 81-7141-524-5.

Vol. 3 *HIV/AIDS—Socio Economic Realities*. ISBN 81-7141-524-3.

Vol. 4 *HIV/AIDS—Law Ethics and Human Rights*, 2 parts. ISBN 81-7141-526-1.

Vol. 5 *AIDS and NGOs*. ISBN 81-7141-527-X.

Vol. 6 *AIDS and Home Care*. ISBN 81-7141-528-8.

Vol. 7 *STD Case Management*. ISBN 81-7141-529-6.

Vol. 8 *HIV/AIDS Prevention and Care—Teaching Modules for Nurses and Midwives*. ISBN 81-7141-530-X.

Vol. 9 *HIV Prevention Education for Educational Institutions*. ISBN 81-7141-531-8.

Vol.10 *Instructional Modules for AIDS Education*. ISBN 81-7141-532-6.

Vol.11 *School Health Education to prevent AIDS and STD—A Package for Curriculum Planners*. ISBN 81-7141-533-4.

Bhaskara Rao, Digumarti, editor (2000). *International Encyclopaedia of Science and Technology Education*, 11 volumes. New Delhi: Discovery Publishing House. ISBN 81-7141-548-2 (set).

Vol. 1 *Science and Technology Education*. ISBN 81-7141-568-7.

Vol. 2 *Science Education in Developing Countries*. ISBN 81-7141-569-9.

Vol. 3 *Organizational Structure of Science*. ISBN 81-7141-570-9.

Vol. 4 *Science Education in Asia and the Pacific*. ISBN 81-7141-571-7

Vol. 5 *Science and Technology Education For All*. ISBN 81-7141-572-5.

Vol. 6 *Values, Ethics, Talent and Girls in Science and Technology Education*. ISBN 81-7141-573-3.

Vol. 7 *Popularization of Science and Technology Education*. ISBN 81-7141-574-1.

Vol. 8 *Science, Power and Society*. ISBN 81-7141-575-X.

Vol. 9 *Information Technology*. ISBN 81-7141-576-8.

Vol. 10 *Teacher Training in Science and Technology Education*. ISBN 81-7142-577-6.

Vol. 11 *Teacher Training in Science and Technology: A Curriculum Framework*. ISBN 81-7141-578-4.

Bhaskara Rao, Digumarti, editor (2001). *Distance Education in Different Countries*. New Delhi: APH Publishing Corporation. ISBN 81-7648-229-3.

Bhaskara Rao, Digumarti, editor (2001). *Decentralised Management of Education: Management of Education in Panchayati Raj and Municipal Bodies*. New Delhi: Discovery Publishing House. ISBN 81-7141-617-9.

Bhaskara Rao, Digumarti, editor (2001). *Electrochemistry for Environmental Protection*. New Delhi: Discovery Publishing House. ISBN 81-7141-619-5.

Bhaskara Rao, Digumarti, editor (2001). *Global Educational Studies*. New Delhi: Discovery Publishing House. ISBN 81-7141-616-0.

Bhaskara Rao, Digumarti, editor (2001). *Global Synthesis of Educational Assessment*. New Delhi: Discovery Publishing House. ISBN 81-7141-613-6.

Bhaskara Rao, Digumarti, editor (2000). *International Encyclopaedia of Human Rights*, 7 volumes in 13 parts. New Delhi: Discovery Publishing House. ISBN 81-7141-567-9 (set).

Vol. 1 *International Instruments of Human Rights*, 2 parts. ISBN 81-7141-569-4.

Vol. 2 *Regional Instruments of Human Rights*. ISBN 81-7141-604-7.

Vol. 3 *Human Rights and the United Nations*, 2 parts. ISBN 81-7141-605-5.

Vol. 4 *Fact Files of Human Rights*, 3 parts. ISBN 81-7141-606-3.

Vol. 5 *Study Stories of Human Rights*, 3 parts. ISBN 81-7141-607-3.

Vol. 6 *International Meetings on Human Rights*, 2 parts. ISBN 81-714-608-X.

Vol. 7 *Professional Training in Human Rights*. ISBN 81-7141-609-8.

Bhaskara Rao, Digumarti, editor (2001). *Jomtein Decade of Education*. New Delhi: Discovery Publishing House. ISBN 81-7141-618-7.

Bhaskara Rao, Digumarti, editor (2001). *Nuclear Materials: Issues and Concerns*, 2 volumes. New Delhi: Discovery Publishing House. ISBN 81-7141-611-X.

Bhaskara Rao, Digumarti, editor (2001). *World Conference on Education for All*. New Delhi: APH Publishing Corporation. ISBN 81-7141-274-9.

Bhaskara Rao, Digumarti, editor (2001). *World Conference on Higher Education*. New Delhi: Discovery Publishing House. ISBN 81-7141-610-1.

Bhaskara Rao, Digumarti, editor (2001). *World Conference on Science*. New Delhi: Discovery Publishing House. ISBN 81-7141-612-8.

Bhaskara Rao, Digumarti, editor (2003). *Inspiring Experiences in Teacher Education*. New Delhi: Discovery Publishing House. ISBN 81-7141-656-X.

Bhaskara Rao, Digumarti, editor (2003). *International Studies in Education*, 3 volumes. New Delhi: Discovery Publishing House. ISBN 81-7141-647-0.

Bhaskara Rao, Digumarti, editor (2003). *Military Conversion: Impact on Science and Technology*. New Delhi: Discovery Publishing House. ISBN 81-7141-578-4.

Bhaskara Rao, Digumarti, editor (2003). *United Nations Millennium Summit*. New Delhi: Discovery Publishing House. ISBN 81-7141-632-2.

Bhaskara Rao, Digumarti, editor (2003). *World Assembly on Aging. New Delhi*: Discovery Publishing House. ISBN 81-7141-637-3.

Bhaskara Rao, Digumarti, editor (2003). *World Conference on Human Rights*. New Delhi: Discovery Publishing House. ISBN 81-7141-661-6.

Bhaskara Rao, Digumarti, editor (2003). *World Education Forum*. New Delhi: Discovery Publishing House. ISBN 81-7141-639-X.

Bhaskara Rao, Digumarti, editor (2003). *Education, Employment and Human Resource Development*. New Delhi: Discovery Publishing House. ISBN 81-7141-681-0.

Bhaskara Rao, Digumarti, editor (2003). *Successful Schooling*. New Delhi: Discovery Publishing House. ISBN 81-7141-677-2.

Bhaskara Rao, Digumarti, editor (2003). *European Education and Teachers*. New Delhi: Discovery Publishing House. ISBN 81-7141-702-7.

Bhaskara Rao, Digumarti, editor (2003). *Teachers in a Changing World*. New Delhi: Discovery Publishing House. ISBN 81-7141-694-2.

Bhaskara Rao, Digumarti, editor (2004). *International Encyclopaedia of Learning to Live Together*, 4 volumes. New Delhi: Discovery Publishing House. ISBN 81-7141-848-1.

Vol. 1 *International Conference on Learning to Live Together.*

Vol. 2 *Globalization and Living Together.*

Vol. 3 *Curriculum for Learning to Live Together.*

Vol. 4 *Science Education for the Contemporary Society.*

Bhaskara Rao, Digumarti, editor (2004). *International Guidelines on Open and Distance Teacher Education*. New Delhi: Discovery Publishing House. ISBN 81-7141-777-9.

Bhaskara Rao, Digumarti, editor (2004). *Adult Learning in the 21st Century*. New Delhi: Discovery Publishing House. ISBN 81-7141-797-3.

Bhaskara Rao, Digumarti, editor (2004). *Educational Practices: Research and Recommendations*. New Delhi: Discovery Publishing House. ISBN 81-7141-835-X.

Bhaskara Rao, Digumarti, editor (2004). *General Secondary Education In the 21st Century*. New Delhi: Discovery Publishing House. ISBN 81-7141-885-6.

Bhaskara Rao, Digumarti, editor (2004). *Reforming Secondary Education*. New Delhi: Discovery Publishing House. ISBN 81-7141-843-0.

Bhaskara Rao, Digumarti, editor (2004). *Human Rights Education*. New Delhi: Discovery Publishing House. ISBN 81-7141-882-1.

Bhaskara Rao, Digumarti, editor (2004). *United Nations Decade for Human Rights Education*. New Delhi: Discovery Publishing House. ISBN 81-7141-887-2.

Bhaskara Rao, Digumarti and B.S.V. Dutt, editors (2003). *Education: Programmes and Policies*. New Delhi: APH Publishing Corporation. ISBN 81-7648-470-9.

Bhaskara Rao, Digumarti, C.A.P. Swamy and B.S.V. Dutt (1997). *Self-Evaluation in Student Teaching*. New Delhi: Discovery Publishing House. ISBN 81-7141-374-9.

Bhaskara Rao, Digumarti and D. Naresh Kumar (2004). *School Teacher Effectiveness*. New Delhi: Discovery Publishing House. ISBN 81-7141-782-5.

Bhaskara Rao, Digumarti and D. Sridhar (2002). *Job Satisfaction of School Teachers*. New Delhi: Discovery Publishing House. ISBN 81-7141-652-7.

Bhaskara Rao, Digumarti, C. Sridevi and K. Vijaya (1995). *Achievement in Social Studies*. New Delhi: Discovery Publishing House. ISBN 81-7141-281-5.

Bhaskara Rao, Digumarti and Digumarti Pushpa Latha (1994). *Achievement in Biology*. New Delhi: Discovery Publishing House. ISBN 81-7141-264-5.

Bhaskara Rao, Digumarti and Digumarti Pushpa Latha (1995). *Achievement in English*. New Delhi: Discovery Publishing House. ISBN 81-7141-283-1.

Bhaskara Rao, Digumarti and Digumarti Pushpa Latha (1994). *Achievement in Science*. New Delhi: Discovery Publishing House. ISBN 81-7141-280-70.

Bhaskara Rao, Digumarti and Digumarti Pushpa Latha (1995). *Achievement in Mathematics*. New Delhi: Discovery Publishing House. ISBN 81-7141-278-5.

Bhaskara Rao, Digumarti and Digumarti Pushpa Latha (2004). *Education for Women*. New Delhi: Discovery Publishing House. ISBN 81-7141-873-2.

Bhaskara Rao, Digumarti and Digumarti Pushpa Latha, editors (1998). *International Encyclopaedia of Women*, 5 volumes. New Delhi: Discovery Publishing House. ISBN 81-7141-410-9 (set).

Vol. 1 *Status of World's Women*. ISBN 81-7141-494-X.

Vol. 2 *Women, Education and Empowerment*. ISBN 81-7141-498-1.

Vol. 3 *Women Challeng:s and Advancement*. ISBN 81-7141-497-4.

Vol. 4 *Women and Family Health*. ISBN 81-7141-497-4.

Vol. 5 *Women and International Action*. ISBN 81-7141-498-2.

Bhaskara Rao, Digumarti, Digumarti Pushpa Latha and Digumarthi Harshitha, editors (2001). *Biological Warfare*. New Delhi: Discovery Publishing House. ISBN 81-7141-597-0.

Bhaskara Rao, Digumarti, Digumarti Pushpa Latha and Digumarthi Harshitha, editors (2001). *Women as Educators*. New Delhi: Discovery Publishing House. ISBN 81-7141-602-0.

Bhaskara Rao, Digumarti and Digumarthi Harshitha (2004). *Adjustment of Adolescents*. New Delhi: APH Publishing House. ISBN 81-7648-836-8.

Bhaskara Rao, Digumarti and Digumarthi Harshitha, editors (2001). *Education in India*. New Delhi: APH Publishing House. ISBN 81-7648-207-2.

Bhaskara Rao, Digumarti, Digumarti Pushpa Latha and Digumarthi Harshitha, editors (2001). *Assessing Learning Achievement*. New Delhi: Discovery Publishing House. ISBN 81-7141-601-2.

Bhaskara Rao, Digumarti, Digumarti Pushpa Latha and Digumarthi Harshitha, editors (2001). *Energy Security*. New Delhi: Discovery Publishing House. ISBN 81-7141-598-9.

Bhaskara Rao, Digumarti, Digumarthi Harshitha and K.R.S. Sambasiva Rao, editors (1999). *Advanced Biotechnology*. New Delhi: Discovery Publishing House. ISBN 81-7141-516-4.

Bhaskara Rao, Digumarti and K.R.S.Sambasiva Rao, editors (1996). *Current Trends in Indian Education*. New Delhi: Discovery Publishing House. ISBN 81-7141-311-0.

Bhaskara Rao, Digumarti and D. Naresh Kumar (2004). *School Teacher Effectiveness*. New Delhi: Discovery Publishing House. ISBN 81-7141-782-5.

Bhaskara Rao, Digumarti and E. Sreekanth Babu (2004). *Educational Interests of School Students*. New Delhi: Discovery Publishing House. ISBN 81-7141-837-6.

Bhaskara Rao, Digumarti and K. Vijaya (1995). *A Text Book Evaluation*. Ambala Cantt: The Associated Publishers.

Bhaskara Rao, Digumarti and M.A. Fayaz (2004). *Problems of Primary School Drop-outs*. New Delhi: Discovery Publishing House. ISBN 81-7141-834-1.

Bhaskara Rao, Digumarti and N.V.M. Mohana Rao (2002). *Problems of Mentally Handicapped Children*. New Delhi: Discovery Publishing House. ISBN 81-7141-645-4.

Bhaskara Rao, Digumarti and S. Chandra Mohan (2002). *Sports Management*. New Delhi: APH Publishing House. ISBN 81-7648-467-9.

Bhaskara Rao, Digumarti and S.A. Khader (2004). *Problems of Private School Teachers*. New Delhi: Discovery Publishing Corporation. ISBN 81-7141-838-4.

Bhaskara Rao, Digumarti and S.A. Khader (2004). *School Education in India*. New Delhi: Discovery Publishing Corporation. ISBN 81-7141-849-X.

Bhaskara Rao, Digumarti and Sk. Johni Basha (2004). *Teachers' Population Education Awareness*. New Delhi: Discovery Publishing House. ISBN 81-7141-832-5.

Bhaskara Rao, Digumarti, V.V. Rao, V.V. Lakshmi and V.V. Krishna, editors (1999). *Status and Advancement of Women*. New Delhi: APH Publishing Corporation. ISBN 81-7648-169-6.

Babu, P.C., author and Digumarti Bhaskara Rao, editor (2004). *Flowers of Wisdom*. New Delhi: Discovery Publishing House. ISBN 81-7141-695-0.

Amala, P.A. and Anupam, P., authors and Digumarti Bhaskara Rao, editor (2004). *History of Education*. New Delhi: Discovery Publishing House. ISBN 81-7141-860-0.

Babu, P.C., author and Digumarti Bhaskara Rao, editor (2005). *Worlds of Wisdom*. New Delhi: Discovery Publishing House. ISBN 81-7141-

Bhagya Lakshmi, L., author and Digumarti Bhaskara Rao, editor (2000). *Reading and Comprehension*. New Delhi: Discovery Publishing House. ISBN 81-7141-543-1.

Bhasha, S.A., author and Digumarti Bhaskara Rao, editor (2004). *Methods of Teaching Geography*. New Delhi: Discovery Publishing House. ISBN 81-7141-807-4.

Bhuvaneswara Lakshmi, Gadde, author and Digumarti Bhaskara Rao, editor (2000). *Attitude Towards Science*. New Delhi: Discovery Publishing House. ISBN 81-7141-541-6.

Bhuvaneswari Lakshmi, G., author and Digumarti Bhaskara Rao, editor (2004). *Methods of Teaching Life Science*. New Delhi: Discovery Publishing House. ISBN 81-7141-804-X.

Bhuvaneswari Lakshmi, G. and K. Subba Rao, authors and Digumarti Bhaskara Rao, editor (2004). *Methods of Teaching Biology*. New Delhi: Discovery Publishing House. ISBN 81-7141-914-3.

Chowdary, S.B.J.R. and Naga Raju authors and Digumarti Bhaskara Rao, editor (2004). *Mastery of Teaching Skills*. New Delhi: Discovery Publishing House. ISBN 81-7141-861-9.

Devraj, T.A.S., author and Digumarti Bhaskara Rao, editor (1997). *Trace Analysis of Uranium and Thorium*. New Delhi: Discovery Publishing House. ISBN 81-7141-375-7.

Durga Rani, K., author and Digumarti Bhaskara Rao, editor (2000). *Educational Aspirations and Scientific Attitudes*. New Delhi: Discovery Publishing House. ISBN 81-7141-555-5.

Dutt, B.S.V. and Digumarti Bhaskara Rao (2001). *Empowering Primary Teachers*. New Delhi: Discovery Publishing House. ISBN 81-7141-615-2.

Dutt, B.S.V., author and Digumarti Bhaskara Rao, editor (2004). *Comparative Education*. New Delhi: Discovery Publishing House. ISBN 81-7141-912-7.

Ediger, Marlow and Digumarti Bhaskara Rao (1996). *Science Curriculum*. New Delhi: Discovery Publishing House. ISBN 81-7141-321-8.

Ediger, Marlow and Digumarti Bhaskara Rao (2000). *Teaching Mathematics Successfully*. New Delhi: Discovery Publishing House. ISBN 81-7141-552-0.

Ediger, Marlow and Digumarti Bhaskara Rao (2001). *Teaching Science Successfully*. New Delhi: Discovery Publishing House. ISBN 81-7141-600-4.

Ediger, Marlow and Digumarti Bhaskara Rao (2001). *Teaching Social Studies Successfully*. New Delhi: Discovery Publishing House. ISBN 81-7141-596-2.

Ediger, Marlow and Digumarti Bhaskara Rao (2002). *Philosophy and Curriculum*. New Delhi: Discovery Publishing House. ISBN 81-7141-631-4.

Ediger, Marlow and Digumarti Bhaskara Rao (2002). *Improving School Administration*. New Delhi: Discovery Publishing House. ISBN 81-7141-633-0.

Ediger, Marlow and Digumarti Bhaskara Rao (2002). *Elementary Curriculum*. New Delhi: Discovery Publishing House. ISBN 81-7141-658-6.

Ediger, Marlow and Digumarti Bhaskara Rao (2003). *Language Arts Curriculum*. New Delhi: Discovery Publishing House. ISBN 81-7141-657-8.

Ediger, Marlow and Digumarti Bhaskara Rao (2003). *Psychology and Curriculum*. New Delhi: Discovery Publishing House. ISBN 81-7141-691-8.

Ediger, Marlow and Digumarti Bhaskara Rao (2003). *Teaching Language Arts Successfully*. New Delhi: Discovery Publishing House. ISBN 81-7141-678-0.

Ediger, Marlow and Digumarti Bhaskara Rao (2003). *School Curriculum and Administration*. New Delhi: Discovery Publishing House. ISBN 81-7141-709-4.

Ediger, Marlow and Digumarti Bhaskara Rao (2003). *Teaching Mathematics in Elementary Schools*. New Delhi: Discovery Publishing House. ISBN 81-7141-687-X.

Ediger, Marlow and Digumarti Bhaskara Rao (2003). *Teaching Science in Elementary Schools*. New Delhi: Discovery Publishing House. ISBN 81-7141-698-5.

Ediger, Marlow and Digumarti Bhaskara Rao (2003). *School Curriculum and Administration*. New Delhi: Discovery Publishing House. ISBN 81-7141-709-4.

Ediger, Marlow and Digumarti Bhaskara Rao (2003). *Elementary Curriculum Improvement*. New Delhi: Discovery Publishing House. ISBN 81-7141-740-X.

Ediger, Marlow and Digumarti Bhaskara Rao (2004). *School Organisation*. New Delhi: Discovery Publishing House. ISBN 81-7141-843-0.

Ediger, Marlow and Digumarti Bhaskara Rao (2004). *Relevancy in Elementary Curriculum*. New Delhi: Discovery Publishing House. ISBN 81-7141-845-9.

Ediger, Marlow, B.S.V. Dutt and Digumarti Bhaskara Rao (2003). *Teaching English Successfully*. New Delhi: Discovery Publishing House. ISBN 81-7141-707-8.

Elizabeth, M.E.S., author and Digumarti Bhaskara Rao, editor (2004). *Methods of Teaching English*. New Delhi: Discovery Publishing House. ISBN 81-7141-809-0.

Harshitha, D. author and Digumarti Bhaskara Rao, editor (2004). *Methods of Teaching Information Technology*. New Delhi: Discovery Publishing House. ISBN 81-7141-805-8.

Indira Devi, author and J. Prasanth Kumar and Digumarti Bhaskara Rao, editors (2004). *Values in Language Text Books*. New Delhi: APH Publishing Corporation. ISBN 81-7141-833-3.

Jalaja Kumari, C., author and Digumarti Bhaskara Rao, editor (2004). *Methods of Teaching Educational Technology*. New Delhi: Discovery Publishing House. ISBN 81-7141-810-4.

Jayasree, Kandi, author and Digumarti Bhaskara Rao, editor (1999). *Correlates of Socialisation*. New Delhi: Discovery Publishing House. ISBN 81-7141-517-2.

Jayasree, Kandi, author and Digumarti Bhaskara Rao, editor (2004). *Methods of Teaching Science*. New Delhi: Discovery Publishing House. ISBN 81-7141-801-5.

John Babu, Chikati, author and T.J.R. Prasad, G.M. Madhukar and Digumarti Bhaskara Rao, editors (1996). *Problem Solving in Mathematics*. New Delhi: APH Publishing Corporation. ISBN 81-7648-273-0.

Joseph Raju, B and G.A. Anitha, authors and Digumarti Bhaskara Rao, editor (2004). *Population Education*. New Delhi: Sonali Publications. ISBN 81-88836-31-3.

Lalitha, T., author and K.S. Prabhakaram, D.S.N. Sastry and Digumarti Bhaskara Rao, editors (2004). *Educational Philosophic Beliefs*. New Delhi: Discovery Publishing House. ISBN 81-7141-765-5.

Madhu Bala, Jampala, author and Digumarti Bhaskara Rao, editor (2004). *Adjustment Problems of Hearing Impaired*. New Delhi: Discovery Publishing House. ISBN 81-7141-831-7.

Madhu Bala, Jampala, author and Digumarti Bhaskara Rao, editor (2004). *Methods of Teaching Exceptional Children*. New Delhi: Discovery Publishing House. ISBN 81-7141-802-3.

Marja, Talvi and Digumarti Bhaskara Rao, editors (1996). *Educational Leadership and Social Changes*. New Delhi: Discovery Publishing House. ISBN 81-7141-320-X.

Nageswara Rao, S. and M. Srihari, authors and Digumarti Bhaskara Rao, editor (2004). *Guidance and Counselling*. New Delhi: Discovery Publishing House. ISBN 81-7141-840-6.

Nageswara Rao, S. and P. Sridhar, authors and Digumarti Bhaskara Rao, editor (2004). *Methods and Techniques of Teaching*. New Delhi: Sonali Publications. ISBN 81-88836-33-8.

Nirmala Jyothi, M., author and Digumarti Bhaskara Rao, editor (2003). *Non-detention System in School Education*. New Delhi: Discovery Publishing House. ISBN 81-7141-654-3.

Padma Tulasi, G., author and Digumarti Bhaskara Rao, editor (2004). *Methods of Teaching Elementary Science*. New Delhi: Discovery Publishing House. ISBN 81-7141-871-6.

Pala Prasada Rao, V., author and K. Nirupa Rani and Digumarti Bhaskara Rao, editors (2004). *Methods of Teaching Elementary Science*. New Delhi: Discovery Publishing House. ISBN 81-7141-871-6.

Prabhakaram, K.S., author and Digumarti Bhaskara Rao, editors (1998). *Concept Attainment Model in Mathematics Teaching*. New Delhi: Discovery Publishing House. ISBN 81-7141-424-9.

Prasanth Kumar, J., author and Digumarti Bhaskara Rao, editor (1998). *Effectiveness of Distance Education System*. New Delhi: Discovery Publishing House. ISBN 81-7141-437-0.

Prasanth Kumar, J., author and Digumarti Bhaskara Rao, editor (2004). *Methods of Teaching Civics*. New Delhi: Discovery Publishing House. ISBN 81-7141-806-6.

Prasanth Kumar, J., author and G. Sundara Rao and Digumarti Bhaskara Rao, editors (2000). *Open University Student Support Services*. New Delhi: Discovery Publishing House. ISBN 81-7141-550-4.

Raja Kumari, M.A. and D.R.S. Sundari, authors and Digumarti Bhaskara Rao, editor (2004). *Special Education*. New Delhi: Discovery Publishing House. ISBN 81-7141-846-5.

Raja Kumari, M.A. and D.R.S. Sundari, authors and Digumarti Bhaskara Rao, editor (2004). *Methods of Teaching Educational Psychology*. New Delhi: Discovery Publishing House. ISBN 81-7141-820-1.

Ramatulasamma, K., author and Digumarti Bhaskara Rao, editor (2002). *Job Satisfaction of Teacher Educators*. New Delhi: Discovery Publishing House. ISBN 81-7141-655-1.

Rama Krishnaiah, D., author and Digumarti Bhaskara Rao, editor (1998). *Job Satisfaction of College Teachers*. New Delhi: Discovery Publishing House. ISBN 81-7141-438-9.

Rama Kumar Ratnam, M.V., author and Digumarti Bhaskara Rao, editor (1998). *Dukkha: Suffering in Early Buddhism*. New Delhi: Discovery Publishing House. ISBN 81-7141-653-5.

Rama Krishna Prasad and P. Vide Sagar, authors and Digumarti Bhaskara Rao, editor (2004). *Methods of Teaching Physical Education*. New Delhi: Discovery Publishing House. ISBN 81-7141-868-6.

Rama Seshaiah, P. author and Digumarti Bhaskara Rao, editor (2004). *Methods of Teaching Home Science*. New Delhi: Discovery Publishing House. ISBN 81-7141-916-X.

Ramesh, Ganta and Digumarti Bhaskara Rao, editors (1998). *Environmental Education: Problems and Prospects*. New Delhi: Discovery Publishing House. ISBN 81-7141-423-0.

Ranga Rao, R., author and Digumarti Bhaskara Rao, editor (2004). *Methods of Teacher Teaching*. New Delhi: Discovery Publishing House. ISBN 81-7141-812-0.

Rathaiah, Lavu and Digumarti Bhaskara Rao, editors (1996), *International Innovations in Education*. New Delhi: Discovery Publishing House. ISBN 81-7141-359-5.

Rathaiah, Lavu and Digumarti Bhaskara Rao (1997). *Achievement Correlates*. New Delhi: Discovery Publishing House. ISBN 81-7141-385-4.

Ravi Krishna, M., author and Digumarti Bhaskara Rao, editor (2004). *Examination System*. New Delhi: Discovery Publishing House. ISBN 81-7141-824-4.

Ravi Kumar, M., author and Digumarti Bhaskara Rao, editor (2004). *Methods of Teaching Computer Science*. New Delhi: Discovery Publishing House. ISBN 81-7141-823-6.

Reddy, Sudhakar Y., author and Digumarti Bhaskara Rao, editor (2003). *Creativity in Adolescents*. New Delhi: Discovery Publishing House. ISBN 81-7141-659-4.

Reddy, M. S., author and Digumarti Bhaskara Rao, editor (2004). *Creativity in College Students*. New Delhi: Discovery Publishing House. ISBN 81-7141-697-7.

Rudramamba, B., author and Digumarti Bhaskara Rao, editor (2003). *Problems of Teaching*. New Delhi: APH Publishing Corporation. ISBN 81-7648-462-8.

Rudramamba, B. and V. Lakshmi Kumari, authors and Digumarti Bhaskara Rao, editor (2004). *Methods of Teaching Economics*. New Delhi: Discovery Publishing House. ISBN 81-7141-900-3.

Sanjeeva Rao, P.C., author and Digumarti Bhaskara Rao, editor (1996). *A Text Book of Geology*. New Delhi: Discovery Publishing House. ISBN 81-7141-313-7.

Satya Narayana, V., author and Digumarti Bhaskara Rao, editor (2001). *Physical Education, Social Attitudes and Leadership Qualities*. New Delhi: Discovery Publishing House. ISBN 81-7141-593-8.

Satya Narayana, P.V.V. and G. Krishna, authors and Digumarti Bhaskara Rao, editor (2004). *Curriculum Development and Management*. New Delhi: Discovery Publishing House. ISBN 81-7141-813-9.

Siva Lakshmi, G.V. and G.L. Subbaiah, authors and Digumarti Bhaskara Rao, editor (2004). *Methods of Teaching Environmental Science*. New Delhi: Discovery Publishing House. ISBN 81-7141-839-2.

Srinivas, M. and I. Prasada Rao, authors and Digumarti Bhaskara Rao, editor (2004). *Methods of Teaching History*. New Delhi: Discovery Publishing House. ISBN 81-7141-803-1.

Srinivasulu Reddy, M. and K.R.S. Sambasiva Rao, authors and Digumarti Bhaskara Rao, editor (1999). *A Text Book of Aquaculture*. New Delhi: Discovery Publishing House. ISBN 81-7141-482-6.

Srinivasa Rao, Mandalapu, author and Digumarti Bhaskara Rao, editor (2003). *Achievement Motivation and Achievement in Mathematics*. New Delhi: Discovery Publishing House. ISBN 81-7141-674-8.

Sunil Kumar, K. and K. Rama Krishana, authors and Digumarti Bhaskara Rao, editor (2004). *Methods of Teaching Chemistry*. New Delhi: Discovery Publishing House. ISBN 81-7141-913-5.

Sunita, E. and R. Sambasiva Rao, authors and Digumarti Bhaskara Rao, editor (2004). *Methods of Teaching Mathematics*. New Delhi: Discovery Publishing House. ISBN 81-7141-915-1.

Swarupa Rani, T. and J.R. Priyadarshini, authors and Digumarti Bhaskara Rao, editor (2004). *Educational Measurement and Evaluation*. New Delhi: Discovery Publishing House. ISBN 81-7141-859-7.

Vanaja, M., author and Digumarti Bhaskara Rao, editor (1999). *Inquiry Training Model*. New Delhi: Discovery Publishing House. ISBN 81-7141-515-6.

Vanaja,M., author and Digumarti Bhaskara Rao, editor (2004). *Methods of Teaching Physics*. New Delhi: Discovery Publishing House. ISBN 81-7141-867-8.

Valeri V. Koustiouk, author and Digumarti Bhaskara Rao, editor (2002). *A Text Book of Cryogenics*. New Delhi: Discovery Publishing House. ISBN 81-7141-642-X.

Vamsi Krishana, V., author and Digumarti Bhaskara Rao, editor (2004). *School Psychology*. New Delhi: Discovery Publishing House. ISBN 81-7141-880-5.

Veena Kumari, Balusu and Digumarti Bhaskara Rao (1996). *Operation Black Board*. New Delhi: APH Publishing Corporation. ISBN 81-7024-711-X.

Veena Kumari, B. author and Digumarti Bhaskara Rao, editor (2004). *Methods of Teaching Social Studies*. New Delhi: Discovery Publishing House. ISBN 81-7141-899-6.

Veena Kumari, Balusu, author and Digumarti Bhaskara Rao, editor (2000). *Psycho-Social Correlates of Achievement*. New Delhi: Discovery Publishing House. ISBN 81-7141-547-4.

Venkata Rao, P. and Digumarti Bhaskara Rao (1989). *A Text Book of Zoology—Junior Intermediate*. Guntur: Vignan Publishers.

Venkata Rao, P. and Digumarti Bhaskara Rao (1989). *A Text Book of Zoology-Senior Intermediate*. Guntur: Vignan Publishers.

Venkateswara Reddy, L. and Lakshmi Narayana, M., authors and Digumarti Bhaskara Rao, editor (2004). *Methods of Teaching Rural Sociology*. New Delhi: Discovery Publishing House. ISBN 81-7141-811-2.

Venkateswara Rao, V., author and Digumarti Bhaskara Rao, editor (2004). *Problems of Education*. New Delhi: Discovery Publishing House. ISBN 81-7141-841-4.

Venkateswara Rao, V., V. Vijaya Lakshmi and V. Vamsi Krishna, authors and Digumarti Bhaskara Rao, editor (2004). *Education For All*. New Delhi: Sonali Publications. ISBN 81-88836-30-3.

Venkateswara Rao, V., V. Vijaya Lakshmi and V. Vamsi Krishna, authors and Digumarti Bhaskara Rao, editor (2004). *Education in India*. New Delhi: Sonali Publications. ISBN 81-88836-858-9.

Venkateswara Reddy, L. and Lakshmi Narayana, M., authors and Digumarti Bhaskara Rao, editor (2004). *Education for Dalits*. New Delhi: Discovery Publishing House. ISBN 81-7141-872-4.

Venkateswarlu, K. and S.J. Basha, authors and Digumarti Bhaskara Rao, editor (2004). *Methods of Teaching Commerce.* New Delhi: Discovery Publishing House. ISBN 81-7141-808-2.

Venugopala Rao, K., author and Digumarti Bhaskara Rao, editor (2000). *Teacher Morale in Secondary Schools.* New Delhi: Discovery Publishing House. ISBN 81-7141-551-2.

Vidya, C., author and Digumarti Bhaskara Rao, editor (1996). *A Text Book of Nutrition.* New Delhi: Discovery Publishing House. ISBN 81-7141-309-9.

Vijaya Bharathi, D., author and Digumarti Bhaskara Rao, editor (2000). *Educational Philosophies of Swami Vivekananda and John Dewey.* New Delhi: APH Publishing House. ISBN 81-7648-309-9.

Vijaya Lakshmi, D., author and Digumarti Bhaskara Rao, editor (2004) *Basic Education.* New Delhi: Discovery Publishing House. ISBN 81-7141-881-3.

Books in Telugu Language

Bhaskara Rao, Digumarti (1986). *Dhrushya Sravana Bodhanapakaranalu (Audio Visual Teaching Aids).* Guntur: Nagarjuna Publishers.

Bhaskara Rao, Digumarti (1993). *Jeevasashtra Bodhana (Teaching of Biology).* Guntur: Nagarjuna Publishers.

Bhaskara Rao, Digumarti (1995). *Vignanasasthra Bodhana (Teaching of science)* Guntur: Nagarjuna Publishers.

Bhaskara Rao, Digumarti (1997). *Vidya Manovignana Seshtram (Educational Psychology).* Guntur: Creative Press.

Bhaskara Rao, Digumarti (1998). *DSC Study Material.* Guntur: Nagarjuna Publishers.

Bhaskara Rao, Digumarti (1998). *Upadhyayudu Vidya. (Teacher and Education)* Guntur: Nagarjuna Publishers.

Bhaskara Rao, Digumarti (1998). *Vidya Drukpadalu (Perspectives of Education).* Guntur: Nagarjuna Publishers.

Bhaskara Rao, Digumarti (1999). *EdCET Teaching Aptitude*. Guntur: Nagarjuna Publishers.

Bhaskara Rao, Digumarti (2001). *Bharata Samajamulo Upadyayudu Vidya (Teacher and Education in Emerging Indian Society)*. Guntur: Sri Nagarjuna Publishers.

Bhaskara Rao, Digumarti (2001). *Bhoutika Sastra Bodhana Paddathulu (Methods of Teaching Physical Science)*. Guntur: Sri Nagarjuna Publishers.

Bhaskara Rao, Digumarti (2001). *Jeeva Sastra Bodhana Padhathulu (Methods of Teaching Biology)*. Guntur: Sri Nagarjuna Publishers.

Bhaskara Rao, Digumarti (2001). *Vidya Manovignana Sastram (Educational Psychology)*. Guntur: Sri Nagarjuna Publishers.

Bhaskara Rao, Digumarti (2003). *Patasala Yajamanyam/Paripalana (School Management and Administration)*. Guntur: Sri Nagarjuna Publishers.

Gopala Krishna, G., A. Ramkrishna, K. Subba Rao and Bhaskara Rao, Digumarti (2004). *Jeevasashtra Bodhana Padhatulu (Methods of Teaching of Biological Science)*. Guntur: Sri Nagarjuna Publishers.

Krishna Murthy, V., K.S. Sudheer Reddy and Digumarti Bhaskara Rao (2004). *Vidya Manovignana Sastra Adharalu (Foundations of Educational Psychology)*. Guntur: Sri Nagarjuna Publishers.

Lalini, V., V. Dayakara Reddy, M. Srihari and Digumarti Bhaskara Rao (2004). *Vidya Adharalu (Foundations of Education)*. Guntur: Sri Nagarjuna Publishers.

Subba Rao, K.P., P. Ayodhya and Digumarti Bhaskara Rao (2004). *Patasala Yajamanyam—Vidhya Vyavasthalu (School Management and Systems of Education)*. Guntur: Sri Nagarjuna Publishers.

Sudhakar, V., B. Ravindra Babu, D.S. Kumar and Digumarti Bhaskara Rao (2004). *Vidya Sanketika Sastram-Computer Vidya (Educational Technology and Computer Education)*. Guntur: Sri Nagarjuna Publishers.